" tell me about your picture "

art activities to help children communicate

Janet Carson

Illustrations by Helen M. Smith

DALE SEYMOUR PUBLICATIONS

Cover design: Rachel Gage

DS31101
ISBN 0-86651-550-X

1 2 3 4 5 6 7 8 9 10-MA-95 94 93 92 91

**DALE
SEYMOUR
PUBLICATIONS**
P.O. BOX 10888
PALO ALTO, CA 94303

CONTENTS

FLO

PREFACE

The White House Conference on Children in 1970 produced a report that indicted the American public for "vast neglect of its children."* Cited as factors in this disturbing commentary on American life were the pervasiveness of television, the occupational mobility of adults, and pressures and priorities that downgrade the role of parents. In the ensuing years, these factors and many others have decreased the opportunity and incentive for meaningful contact between children and persons older than they. This book seeks to provide support for those children who, as a result of low communication levels with parents or friends, are unable or reluctant to speak about their thoughts and feelings. Topics of special interest to children have been integrated into art lessons so that youngsters, as they express themselves through the things they make, are eager to talk as well. Lesson helps are as follows:

     1. The skills, knowledge, and interests of children generally differ according to age and grade level. The lessons in this book are headed by large graphic numbers indicating the public-school grade level at which each will be most effective.

     2. Each chapter dwells upon a different subject for expression. Some lessons will inspire sharing about home, family, and friends, whereas others encourage the flow of imagination. There is a chapter that encourages children to experiment, a chapter devoted to drawing

*Report to the President: White House Conference on Children. Washington, D.C.: U.S. Government Printing Office, 1971.

techniques, and one that reveals "tricks" with art media. All the lessons have been tested for their appeal with groups of children by a professional art teacher.

3. It is typical that children maintain a high level of interest in a task for only short periods of time. A change of pace is essential to continued concentration. Thus, "doing" and "talking" time is carefully planned and is shown by a clock face that heads each lesson.

4. A special feature is the clear procedures shown in full-page illustrations.

Most of the materials needed are available at shopping centers or variety stores and through school supply catalogs. For lesson planning purposes, an art learning objective introduces each lesson.

What makes this book unique are the Arttalk questions listed at the end of each lesson. The teacher or leader who uses these questions will find that they will stimulate children to express their ideas in words as well as in art. Directions for using the questions in the course of each lesson are given, as well as tips on how a teacher may show children that he or she really wants to hear what they have to say. Any child reluctant to speak will thus feel encouraged to do so. By incorporating knowledge of children's interests gained over years of working with children, I have chosen questions that children *want* to answer. A sample dialogue might be:

> *Question:* When you leave for school in the morning, do you usually go out the *front* door?
> *Answer:* We go out the *side* door.
> *Question:* Does anybody else use a side door?
> *Answer:* I always go out the *back* door. My mother doesn't want me to use the front door. Our boots are at the back door.

Children in America today are being brought up in a less cohesive, less closely knit family structure than formerly. In this continuing pattern of social change, some children don't receive the attention from parents they once did. Many parents are torn between the desire for personal fulfillment and the responsibilities of rearing children. Video games, music lessons, Little League, television, child care centers, and a host of other diversions provide children with entertainment and learning but deny them the emotional interaction with caring parents that they so desperately need. They miss out on the discussions of feelings, values, and innermost thoughts that can be shared only with people who have the inclination and time to listen. As a result, children may feel cheated and less secure, and their sense of self-worth is diminished.

It has long been acknowledged that art is therapeutic for both old and young. With the addition of probing questions designed to stir children to speak about their ideas, this book, I hope, will be a valuable resource for teachers and volunteers who want to help them.

I wish to acknowledge my recent experience at Canadian Academy, Kobe, Japan, reaffirming a long-felt notion that the making of art heals and helps in many ways. To my good friend Charlotte Hubert, I offer thanks for support and help in the writing of this book.

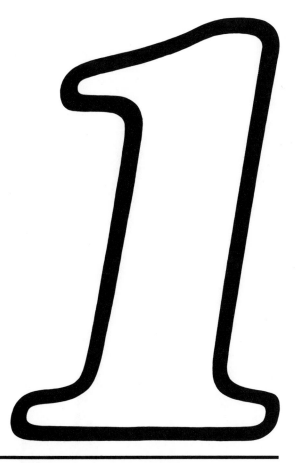

GET READY,
GET SET

AN INVITATION TO SPEAK

This book is written about ways to help children *talk*. Youngsters need encouragement to express opinions and feelings through language. Art lessons in this book have been designed to help children do just that.

Most children like to draw, paint, and work with other art materials. When they have created something on their own, they identify with it. When they are asked to speak about it, the work provides a visual support. It is there for everyone to view. Explaining it or expressing feelings attached to it becomes quite natural and easy, both in and out of school settings.

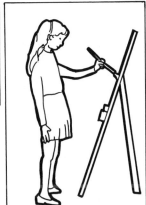

The lessons in this book have been designed to trigger spontaneous verbal discussion or description among children otherwise reluctant to speak. Through their own art, children tend to give *authentic* responses, not ones they have learned from television, from their friends, or ones that they think adults want to hear. Children desperately want to shout to the world.

THIS IS ME! HERE I AM!

Through their art work, their self-image is strengthened.

In the growing number of single-parent households, many breadwinners don't have the time to form intimate relationships with their children as parents once did. Thus, the opportunities for the child to share personal opinions and reflections are fewer. Even in traditional family structures, the full-time role of wife and mother is no longer assumed by most women. Television provides children with one-sided communication and, unfortunately, a seductive substitute for close relationships.

A significant aspect of the American social structure is its mobility. Many children are never in one school long enough to make lasting friendships. Because they are bused, school friends often live far apart, denying them opportunities for after-school companionship. Grandparents, aunts, uncles, and other caring relatives more than likely live miles away.

The arrival of Spanish-speaking people and immigrants from Southeast Asia has flooded our schools with children for whom English is not their primary language. It has been estimated in recent years that in at least twenty percent of American homes a language other than English is spoken. Thus, assimilation through language is an important concern in schools and community support groups.

The lessons in this book are especially valuable for children from ages five to ten (about kindergarten through fourth grade). Before age five, children aren't inclined to listen to one another, and after age ten, children become reluctant to show their art work because of growing concern for peer approval and self-criticism.

"SHOWING THE PICTURE" or other art work to one caring observer is a valuable experience for every child. Showing a picture or art work in a group setting (in school, Scout troops, 4-H, church school, etc.) is more beneficial for the speaker as well as the observer if there is a leader who will set down firm rules for "show and tell."

SHOW AND TELL

When it appears that some of the children are finished with their art work, ask, "Who would like to show their picture?" There is often a flurry of hands or a chorus of "I want to! I want to!"

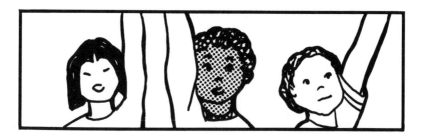

Tell the first volunteer to stand in clear view of all the other children. If the child has a picture to show, the volunteer should hold it high, under the chin, with two hands, so everyone can see. Tell the child to hold the picture *still* and turn *slowly* so everyone can have a first look. Then the child may use one hand to point to various parts of the picture to amplify the explanation. If the art work is three-dimensional, there should be a table nearby to display it.

Announce to the rest of the children that they may continue their work while, one at a time, volunteers come to the front of the group to show. Children have a wonderful facility for working and listening at the same time. If members of the group wish to comment about the work being shown, let this happen naturally. Children are

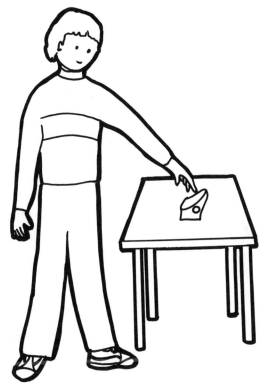

usually quite charitable in this regard if you have established an atmosphere of caring within the group.

In a schoolroom of thirty children who are *all* eager to "show," the teacher has to decide how many minutes can be devoted to this activity. It may be that there is time for only a few children to take a turn. Starting with the "early finishers" during the work period gives more children this chance.

Many children will speak very freely about their pictures. If possible, call on them first. When a child starts speaking, you should move behind the other children and, if necessary, encourage the child

to speak up so you can hear. This will ensure that the rest of the children can hear as well. If you stand next to the child, in front of the others, the child will tend to turn and speak to *you* rather than to the rest of the group.

Tactfully bring lengthy orations to a close so that the more reluctant youngsters will have a chance to speak. For these children you may want to use the Artalk questions at the end of each lesson, beginning at Chapter 8. Be sure to give each child your full attention. *Listen closely* to what is said and give appropriate responses. Vacant answers such as "Isn't that nice" can be interpreted as indifference. Your response must be *authentic* if you expect authenticity from the child.

3

TURNING ON THE SOUND

WHAT KINDS OF LESSONS INSPIRE VERBAL FEEDBACK?

Lessons that spark imagination or fantasy

All children like to make up stories, and in an atmosphere of *trust*, a fantastic drawing or sculpture can inspire the maker to take off on a wonderfully unselfconscious description of the art work. To a child, there is no standard by which such a picture or sculpture can be measured, so every result will be "right." The spirit of fun which surrounds such lessons diminishes fear of failure so that the artist is eager not only to draw or make, but also to "show and tell."

Lessons that allow children to "tell what they know"

Art lessons pertaining to home, family, friends, pets, favorite pastimes, vacations, holiday activities, and games all generate enthusiastic response. The quality of the drawings may be uneven, and the maker may typically say "I can't draw it very good, but . . . ." Because the subject matter is so familiar, the child's verbal response is usually authentic, presenting a prime opportunity for avoiding the typical playground posturing or the desire to impress peers. In other words, the child will tend to speak about what is true—a boon to the development of a healthy self-concept.

Lessons that open doors to new discoveries

Sometimes teachers or volunteers pass up opportunities for helping children become more visually aware of the world around them. Children are excited by new visual discoveries. What child can resist the magic world of a kaleidoscope?

Children can be truly captivated as they more carefully observe lines, shapes, textures, and colors. Lessons designed to emphasize one or more of these elements can often produce stunning

results. Children are surprised and pleased as they become sharply conscious of aesthetic qualities.

The sense of wonder that accompanies these new experiences can inspire children to speak thoughtfully about their art work.

Lessons that teach drawing techniques

These lessons are appropriate for older children, and include specific instruction in shading, overlapping, and other means of achieving three-dimensional effects in drawing or modeling. Children are so filled with a sense of power as they master "life-like" effects, that they may be eager to "show and tell" in spite of peer pressure, at this age, to "stay cool."

Lessons that teach children "tricks" with media

The novelty of a new medium or a new way of handling a familiar medium always inspires interest. Older children who may be taking a jaundiced view of their ability to "do art" (a typical response as they become more self-critical) can become newly inspired by a medium and its application. Sometimes a new medium becomes a "breakthrough" for a child otherwise reluctant because of what is seen as past "failures." At such time there can be a desire to share that excitement with others.

Starting with Chapter 8 there are suggestions for specific lessons under each of the preceding general headings. Each lesson states the time needed to effectively complete the activity, the appropriate age level for the lesson, and the specific art concepts involved, as well as "Artalk" questions to get the discussion started.

TIME IS OF THE ESSENCE

The time needed for sharing results can vary, depending on the age of the child and on the activity. Many little children complete an art task quickly but can talk endlessly about it to anyone who will listen. The length of the sharing time, then, will be influenced partly by the attention span of the listeners. It is important that the sharing commence immediately following the activity, or start while the slower children are finishing, as suggested in Chapter 2. If time is allowed to elapse between the activity and the sharing, the response quickly turns "cold" as younger children forget their initial enthusiasm.

Older children often make a great fuss about getting up in front of a group to show their art work, but are secretly delighted if they are urged to do so. A perceptive teacher or leader must know which children really *mean* it when they balk at taking part in this activity. These children are often willing, however, to let the teacher display their work. A day or two later, the children will retain enough interest in what they have done to take part in a discussion about the work as a whole.

The clock symbol on each of the illustration pages includes the minutes necessary for warm-up or motivation questions, the work period, and the follow-up sharing time. The length of time should be about right if there are between 15 and 25 students.

5

NOT TOO HARD, NOT TOO EASY, BUT JUST RIGHT

Many teachers in public schools proclaim that their students "don't like art" when the real problem is that the activities presented are inappropriate for the children they are teaching. Children balk at lessons they feel they can't handle, and are bored with activities they judge insipid. Attempt to inspire any "Artalk" is then useless.

The choice of art activities should be based on an awareness of a child's physical, social, and psychological growth. There is general agreement on these developmental growth stages, which are linked to grade levels in school. The lessons in this book have been "kitchen tested" in both public and private schools, but have been assigned a number that embraces more than one grade level because of different growth patterns in individual children. This number is located directly above the title of each lesson.

Lessons with the numeral 1 will be most effective for children from five to seven years old. Lessons with the numeral 2 will be most appropriate for children from six to eight years old. Lessons graded 3 will be interesting to children within the range of seven to nine years. Lessons graded 4 will appeal to children from eight to ten years of age.

This numbering scheme may not fit children who are considered gifted or who are hampered either by lack of early experience or with learning disabilities. However, if leaders do not use the numbers as a general guide, they may find that the lesson is not as successful as it could be.

ART LEARNING

Below the title of each lesson, beginning on page 22, there is an indication of "art learning." This phrase refers to the specific art concept the lesson emphasizes. This will be of special interest to teachers intent on identifying art concepts while they provide children with a "soapbox" from which to speak about their work.

People have always used art to express their ideas. Making their own art provides children with insight into themselves, their world; it invites them to look more closely and enjoy the richness of their visual surroundings. Being involved with art helps children discriminate, to choose carefully the colors, shapes, and lines that they will use to make their art. This behavior can become the basis for aesthetic choices in adult life.

ARTALK

Artalk can occur at the beginning, middle, or end of the art activity. Most of the lessons in this book invite feedback from the children *after* they have completed their projects.

The opening discussion period can also provide a rich opportunity for children to express opinions, tell about what they know, or weave a fantastic tale. Sample questions might be:

- Where is your "special place?"
- What happens to the size of a road as it disappears in the distance?
- If you could design a machine to do any kind of work, what would it be?

Questions asking what? where? how? and why? will spark interest and generate an answer if they relate closely to the child's world. Sample questions might be:

- What time do you get up in the morning?
- Where is your favorite place to eat?
- How can you make a person fit in a circle?
- Why did you put your dog in your family picture?

These questions should elicit specific opinions and show the children that you want to know what they *think*.

When posing questions and acknowledging answers, a good

way to support an expressed opinion or statement is to paraphrase what has been said.

> *Question:* What do you like to do on Sunday afternoon?
> *Answer:* Watch football on TV.
> *Response:* So you like to watch football. A Packer fan?
> *Possible interruption:* No!! Minnesota!

or

> *Question:* How many windows are in the front of your house?
> *Answer:* Three windows.
> *Response:* (Teddy) says three windows. How about the rest of you? How many say three?

The more specifically the questions address a child's concerns (family, neighborhood, recent events, sports, weather, TV cartoons, TV games, food, advertising campaigns and jingles), the better. Slant your questions toward a child's interest and there is guaranteed attention and possible response.

"How does this picture make you feel?" may sound like an appropriate question, but in fact, many children find it difficult to talk about feelings. In a group setting it may be too much to expect a child to confess, "It makes me sad," or "I was mad when . . . " Children speak with candor when they have a strong self-image and feel secure. Many of the children whom these lessons will benefit may *not* feel secure, so teachers and leaders need to be alert to expressions of feelings that are perceived through the selective information the child provides. Feelings can also be detected in a note of pride in a child's voice, or in a closed facial expression telling the teacher that the child is uncomfortable. As these subtle indicators are revealed, an astute teacher or leader provides firm support by showing keen interest in what the child is saying "about the picture." This support says to the child, "I am interested in YOU."

Some children are accustomed to being ignored. They have been put aside from speaking so many times at home by busy parents or by competing siblings that they are reluctant to say *anything*. These children won't answer unless addressed directly. Calling a child by name, looking the child fully in the eyes, and *waiting* expectantly, may be all that's needed to produce a response. Consider this response a *gift* and receive it with grace.

GET READY, GET SET, GO

TELL ME ABOUT IDEAS YOU MADE UP

A large part of a little child's awareness is given up to dreaming. Children sometimes need encouragement to share their personal inventions and present a little of their true selves to others. They are willing to share ideas in the form of drawings because they are quite confident the symbols used are appropriate for what they want to show. The viewer may ask, "Would you like to tell me about your picture?" and be promptly bombarded with a torrent of words, describing in detail images that may seem impossible for the mystified adult to decipher.

Older children invent also. Because in an artistic environment ideas that are "made up" are usually considered acceptable, a drawing that may seem imperfect can still be "OK" to the maker because "I didn't *want* it to look real," or "I *meant* it to look funny." Older children are apt to be frustrated easily in their attempts to draw in a way that suits them, and some could easily give up making *anything* in art. Imaginary subjects provide a wider avenue of expression because "anything goes." There is something exhilarating about giving birth to an idea, one that no one else has thought of. The proud owner craves recognition. When pictures are shown, the resulting good-natured exchange can sometimes "break loose" a child who normally chooses to say very little.

TWO CIRCLE PICTURES

Encouraging Perception and Imagination

You'll Need

One piece of 12 × 18 inch newsprint paper for each child, two circles drawn on each sheet, plus a few extras. Circles both large and

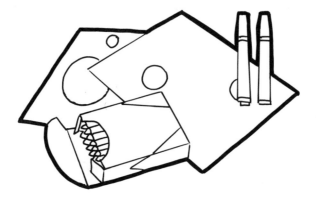

small should be drawn with black marker and placed in different positions on each paper. Each child should have crayons, markers, or oil crayons.

Let's Go

Begin with Artalk questions below. Show a sample paper with the circles drawn on it. Explain to the children that they are to solve a "problem of the circles." Each child is to think of a picture of which the circles will become a part. Each paper will present a different task. Encourage the children to turn their papers any way they wish and take their time to think of good ideas. Refer to some of the circle forms that are suggested in the Artalk questions. Their pictures might be illustrations of stories they make up. Tell them to pay attention to background detail, and make their drawings extend to the edges of the paper. Early finishers may try another picture, but not until the first picture is completed and colored.

Artalk Artalk Artalk Artalk Artalk

Let's each take a turn and name one thing in this room that has a *circle* in it. Now think of something that has a circle in it that we can't see here.

When you have finished, tell us the story of your picture. If you like, you can call on a classmate to come up and point to the circles you started with.

HALLOWEEN SPOOK

Encouraging Imagination and Perception

You'll Need

One double sheet of newspaper taped vertically to an empty wall for each child, black and orange tempera paint thickened with soap flakes, easel-size brushes and a few small detail brushes, smocks for each child.

Let's Go

At Halloween time sit on the floor, and gather the children around you in a group. Ask them to make scary faces. (You make one, too!) Ask those who demonstrate with enthusiasm to turn around and show the others. Some will hunch their shoulders, and hold their hands in claw positions. Eyes may squint, foreheads may wrinkle, feet may turn outward.

Let each child pick a painting spot by a newspaper to make a frightening spook as big as the paper. As the youngsters proceed to the painting area, they can each pick up a small tin of the thick black paint and a large brush. The newspaper on the wall, marked with dark areas of headlines or photographs turned sideways, serves as a background to complement the strong blacks of the shapes and features of each painting. As the children finish painting the black outlines, have the orange paint available with small detail brushes to add accents.

Artalk Artalk Artalk Artalk Artalk

What makes a spook look like a spook? What makes it scary? What happens to your eyes, your mouth, and your hands when you try to appear frightening? Show us your spook and tell us how you tried to make it scary.

ADDING TO A PICTURE

Encouraging Ingenuity and Detail

You'll Need

Manila drawing paper 12 in. × 18 in., scissors, white glue or paste, crayons, cutouts of photographic objects from magazines* (such as a camera, a truck, a lamp, a bottle). These should be cut away from adjoining text or other images, but do not need to be cut close to the edge of the objects. They can be of different sizes, but not larger than 6 in. × 9 in.

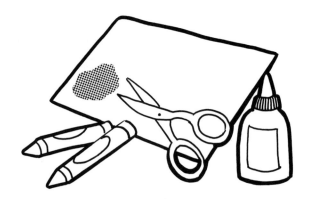

Let's Go

Give each child a cutout object. Ask everyone in the group to cut carefully around the objects they have been given. Using the Artalk questions below, challenge them to think of interesting settings for their objects. Encourage the children to think of details which will help the viewer know exactly where the objects are. When they have taken time to think of a good idea, they should glue their objects where they want them on their papers and add to them using crayons or markers to

---

*Good sources: *Better Homes and Gardens, Time*, weekend supplements in newspapers, any source that has large colored advertisements.

make their pictures interesting. Suggest that the environment for their objects be logical (on a shelf, table, in a garage, in a pocket, etc.) but allow zany locations if they are carefully drawn.

Artalk Artalk Artalk Artalk Artalk

(Hold up one of the cutout objects.) Where could *this* be? Where *else* could it be? (Seek several answers.) What might be *around* it? *Below* it? *Above* it? Would it sit on a table, in a hand, or float in the air? (Hold up another object and repeat similar questions.)

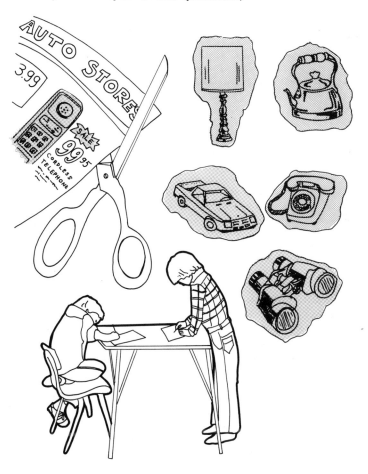

PAPER FASTENER MACHINES

Using Imagination

You'll Need

Variety of colored construction paper 12 in. × 18 in., one paper fastener, colored paper scraps, wax or oil crayons, one tagboard disc 5 in. diameter for each child.

Let's Go

Give each child one piece of the colored construction paper, a tagboard disc, and a paper fastener. Ask three volunteers to stand in front of the group. Give each a specific bodily movement to repeat over and over: 1) crank arms 2) turn around while bobbing head up and down 3) bend knees up and down. Tell them that they are a machine and when you touch the "on" button, the machine will do its work. Turn them "on" and let them continue the motions for half a minute, then turn them "off." After the volunteers have returned to their seats, challenge the children to use their discs, with paper fasteners pushed through the centers and then into some part of their construction papers, to make imaginary machines. The discs might become wheels, connected to other wheels, an engine block, cranks, springs, levers, pistons, belts, switches, spark plugs, or whatever they can think of. The children may use crayons and colored paper scraps to make these additions. Pass out more paper fasteners if they have ideas to make other moving parts.

If the children cannot think of machines, tell them to think of their discs as other circular objects, such as balls, planets, oranges, or phonograph records. They should then make appropriate backgrounds for their machines or other ideas.

Artalk Artalk Artalk Artalk Artalk

What is the name of your machine? Tell us what it does. How does it work? (For the children who chose a different theme): Tell us what you made using your disc. Name the other objects in your picture and tell us about your idea.

A MINIATURE PLAYGROUND

Encouraging Imagination

You'll Need

White tagboard 4 in. × 6 in. for each child, multi-colored construction paper strips 1 in. × 9 in., ½ in. × 9 in., scissors, white glue or paste, colored string, colored paper scraps.

Let's Go

Place piles of the colored strips, the colored string and the paper scraps in a central location. Ask the children to design playground equipment for very tiny people. Pick out one of the colored strips of paper, fold back one end about ½ in. and paste the end down on one of the tagboard pieces so that the rest of the strip sticks up in the air. Show the children how they can loop this strip, twist it, or fold it before they paste the other end down to the base. Tell them to "think tiny." Each child should take just five strips at first. Then, if they need scraps of paper, string, or more strips, they can pick them up after they've worked for a few minutes with their first pieces. If the equipment they make goes too high it will be unstable, so they should be sure to attach the ends of their strips firmly to each other or to the base.

Artalk Artalk Artalk Artalk Artalk

If you were very little, what would be fun to crawl through, climb over or slide down? Show and tell us how you play or do tricks on the equipment you have designed.

loop it   twist it   fold it

ILLUSTRATING A POEM

Encouraging Imagination and Fluency

You'll Need

White drawing paper 12 in. × 18 in., 1 thin-line black marker, a copy of Shel Silverstein, *Where the Sidewalk Ends* (New York: Harper & Row, 1974).

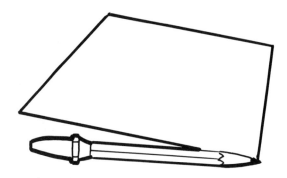

Let's Go

Read the poem "Hungry Mungry" *slowly*. Challenge the children to listen to *every word*, especially for the visual images that are part of the poem. After you have read it through *once*, ask them to begin drawing *without talking* as you begin to read again. Encourage them to draw as many objects as they can to describe what they are hearing.

Artalk Artalk Artalk Artalk Artalk

Tell us about the things you remembered to put in your picture. Which of these things do *you* like to eat? During the reading, when did you decide that "Hungry Mungry" was a silly poem?

DOORS TO . . .

Encouraging Imagination

You'll Need
Manila paper 9 in. × 12 in., crayons.

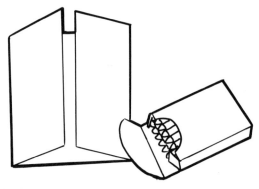

Let's Go

Tell each child to fold the paper in half, open the paper up, then fold each outer edge into the middle. The folds are "doors." Ask the children to name all the types of doors they can think of. Where do doors go? Ask enough children so that answers become increasingly imaginative. Encourage a bit of insanity! The children are to draw and color the details of the closed "doors." When they are finished they may open them up and draw what's inside. Encourage them to take their time and make as many interesting details as they can think of.

Artalk Artalk Artalk Artalk Artalk

What kind of doors have you made? (The child may call on friends to guess what's inside the doors, and then should show and tell about what is inside.)

ALPHABET ANTICS

Encouraging Perception and Imagination

You'll Need
Manila drawing paper 9 in. × 12 in., with letters of the alphabet

printed boldly with black marker, one on each sheet (if there are more than twenty-six children in the group, print numbers as well), crayons or colored markers for each child.

Let's Go

Hold up a sample paper with a letter printed on it. Spend several minutes asking the children what the shape of the letter reminds them of. Tell them to pretend that the shape could be part of something else. Tell them to think of it as something they could look down on, look through, or look up to. Turn the paper in a different direction. Keep asking the children to think of *more* things. As the ideas begin to flow, present the challenge that each of them will be given a letter and that they are to think of several things to make with their shapes before they make a decision. Tell them that artists take a long time to make choices for their art, so they need not hurry. They can add to the shapes they have been given, making an interesting picture. Tell them that whatever they make could project off the page. They can add details appropriate to the settings they have chosen. They can use their crayons or markers to fill in *all* areas of the paper to make the picture complete.

Artalk Artalk Artalk Artalk Artalk

What are some of the ideas you thought of when you first looked at your letter? What made you decide on the subject you chose for your alphabet picture? Show us where the original letter form was. Tell us about the details you added to your picture to make it interesting.

ADD-TO-IT
TRACE YOUR SHOE PICTURE

Encouraging Ingenuity

You'll Need

Manila or newsprint paper 12 in. × 18 in., black thin-line markers, crayons.

Let's Go

Tell each child to take off one of his or her shoes and lay it on the paper in any position. The shoe may be laid flat on the paper, on its side, or positioned partly *off* the paper. When the shoe is placed, it should be traced carefully with the marker. (When they are finished they can put their shoes back on. At this point use Artalk questions listed below.) Tell the children to turn their papers slowly in all four directions. They should take time to study the shape and the space around it. They should use their crayons to make the shoe shape into something else. Tell them to think of the shape as above, below, or inside something. They should resist using their first idea, or even their second. Urge them to think of ideas no one else would think of. They should add details and background around the shape; they may draw things inside the shape if they like. The more details, the more interesting the picture! They should color in the whole space and accent important objects by outlining them with their thin-line markers.

Artalk Artalk Artalk Artalk Artalk

If you didn't know that the shape on your paper was a shoe or part of a shoe, what else could it be? What else? More! Keep thinking! Could it be *part* of something else? That's a good idea! What *else*? Who can think of another idea? If you could add to it, what could it be? (The teacher or leader should keep hammering away. The first ideas will be obvious ones; if the children are urged to really *think*, they will become involved, and more inventive ideas will flow.)

(As the children are finishing) Who is ready to show their picture? Tell us how you finally hit on your idea. Is this idea better than your first one? What would be a good title for your picture? How about taking off your shoe and showing us how you positioned it on your paper!

ALL KINDS OF PEOPLE

Encouraging Imagination and Fluency

You'll Need
Light-colored construction paper in the following shapes and sizes: 5 in. circle, 6 in. square, rectangles 3 in. × 9 in., 4 in. × 6 in., 3 in. × 6 in. (one of each per child), thin-line markers.

Let's Go
Challenge the children to make five different people that fit the five shapes they have been given. Encourage distortion, variety in clothing and in facial features. They may draw environmental details if they can fit them in. Challenge the children to make each character totally different from the next. They should try hard to think of interesting ways to fill each space (big ears, a funny hat, balloons in hand, body bent over, etc.)

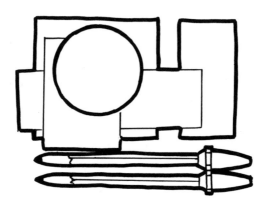

Artalk Artalk Artalk Artalk Artalk

Who is ready to show their five people? Tell about them one at a time. Show us how you made each different from the others. What are their names? Hmm. *That's* a strange name! How did you think of *that*? Which one do you think is your best?

CARTOON STORY

Encouraging Imagination and Perception

You'll Need

White drawing paper 12 in. × 18 in., newsprint 4½ in. × 6 in., five or six wide-mouth jars, pencils, thin-line black markers, scissors.

Let's Go

Arrange the children in groups of four or five, with a jar in the middle of each group. Tell the children to draw the jar on the small piece of newsprint so that it fills the space. When finished, they should cut it out. Then they should fold their white drawing paper into fourths, open it up, and lay it flat so that the longest side runs vertically. They are to trace the cutout of the jar onto three of the four panels, so that the bottle drawing sits on the bottom edge of each panel. In the first panel the bottle should be at the center of the bottom edge, in the second and third panels, near the right side. Leave the fourth panel empty. Challenge the children to draw a "Something" in the bottle struggling to get out.

Artalk Artalk Artalk Artalk Artalk

What have you made in your bottle? Describe its journey to the world outside. What will it do when it gets out?

DESIGNING A NEW CEREAL BOX

Encouraging Imagination and Perception

You'll Need

Empty cereal boxes brought from home (bring extras for those who forget or who do not eat cereal in the morning), 2 pieces 18 in. × 24 in. newsprint (or sheets of similar size torn off a white paper roll for each child), glue, markers, colored paper scraps, scissors, newspapers, masking tape.

Let's Go

Use *Artalk* questions first. Tell the children they should pretend they are artists designing a box to advertise a brand-new cereal. It is their job to invent a new name and design a box that will be appealing to the shopper. The design should be bold and attractive. They should try to think of how several boxes with the same design would look sitting together on a shelf. Direct the children to stuff their cereal boxes with small wads of newspaper so the boxes will not collapse. Seal the boxes with masking tape. Demonstrate how to wrap the cereal boxes like gifts. Be sure that the edges are creased. The children should glue the paper to the boxes. If newsprint is used, a double thickness is necessary so the images on the original boxes won't

show through. Tell the children to draw the letters of their cereal name big and cut them out of colored paper. After these are glued on, they may go around them with markers to make them stand out. Then encourage them to put pictures or other words around the name to enhance the design. Early finishers may want to write messages on the sides of the box or turn the box over and design a box top contest on the back.

Artalk Artalk Artalk Artalk Artalk

How many of you eat breakfast? How many of you like cold cereal? What is your favorite kind? Who can remember what the front of your favorite cereal looks like? How big is the name of the cereal on the box? What other pictures or words are on the box? (At completion) How have you designed your cereal box to attract the shopper's attention?

9

TELL ME ABOUT THINGS YOU KNOW

Children need opportunities to talk to someone about things that are important to them. In our fast-paced society, these opportunities can be few and far between. Some parents rush their children to baseball practice, piano lessons, and a multitude of other activities which are designed to enrich their lives, but in fact, rob the child of making choices, muddling through mistakes, and learning from them. Conversations are on the run. "Call at 5 P.M.!" "Stay out of the mud!" "Don't take off your coat, it isn't *that* warm out!" Other families have allowed television to take so much of their time that conversations become limited to necessary exchanges during three-minute commercials. Many single parents, swamped with multiple roles as breadwinner, housekeeper and home-maintenance person, are not available for other than admonishments, "Don't forget to turn on the oven." "Watch out for your little sister." "If anyone calls, tell them I'll be home at five." A child may feel permitted to utter only the words which are of prime importance. Musings or ruminations, "I wonder if," "I think," "It seems to me" are left unresolved because there is no one to listen.

Children feel comfortable and confident drawing and making things focused on home, family, friends, favorite pastimes, vacations, or holidays.

Warm relationships grow as people share personal thoughts with each other. Within an atmosphere of trust (which an able leader must establish), drawing and making things which have as their focus familiar subjects gives some children a chance, when sharing time comes, to make the first, hesitant attempts to "connect" to a world which otherwise rushes by unconcerned. Beginnings of empathy can start here, as both listener and speaker discover that everyone knows fear and frustration as well as dreams and joys.

DRAWING MY FAMILY

Encouraging Personal Expression

You'll Need

White drawing paper or newsprint 12 in. × 18 in., oil crayons or colored markers, pencils (for writing names).

Let's Go

Use the Artalk questions below. Tell the children to begin drawing the tallest member of the family first, and make that person as big as the paper. Make the head "bump" the top of the paper, with the feet resting on the bottom. Then they are to think of the next tallest, and gradually continue adding people up to the smallest (a baby or family pet). As they draw each person, they should think of how much shorter than the tallest person the next one is.* Encourage them to think of what each person usually wears, and try to show it. They should try to think of distinguishing features which will identify each one—curly hair, glasses, a special necklace, a particular T-shirt, a belt buckle or boots. They may use their pencils to write the names of their family members beside each figure.

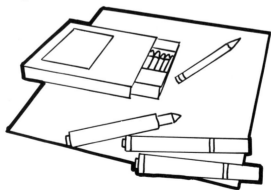

---

*Some children will disregard your instructions and draw sizes according to the feelings they have about each person. Such deviations can provide useful information for teachers or counselors regarding the child's concept of his family members.

Artalk Artalk Artalk Artalk Artalk

Count the number of people in your family. How many people live in your house? Who is the tallest? Who is the littlest? How big are your father or mother when you stand close to them? Does your mother wear pants or a skirt most of the time? Are your father's working clothes different from those he wears when he is watching TV? When you are finished with your pictures, you can tell us about your family.

MY HOUSE*

Encouraging Personal Expression and Recall

You'll Need

Ten pieces each of white, gray, yellow, brown, light green, light blue, red construction paper, 9 in. × 12 in., arranged in piles on a table near the children; crayons, paste or glue, scissors, 6 pieces of 1 in. × 2 in. gray construction paper for each child; a box of colored paper scraps.

Let's Go

From the centrally located table, each child should pick up a piece of paper that most closely resembles the color of his house. When all are seated, ask them to shut their eyes and think about the slant of the roof of the house. Can you see the roof from the front? How much will

*or apartment

long   or   tall

how many windows?

fold   cut

you need to cut off the sides of the paper for the roof? If the roof is flat, you won't need to cut anything. Is your house long or tall? They may turn their paper either direction. How many windows are there in front of the house? The children should count out the correct number of windows and return the rest of the gray rectangles to the central table. Where is the front door? Show them that by cutting an upside down "L" shape they can make a door that opens. Then they may paste down their windows where they belong and color in the trim. Then they will want to make the bushes, trees or whatever is in front of the house, plus the chimney (if they remember where it is). These details can be made with colored scraps pasted down in the proper position. If they can see the roof, or even the edge of it, they can draw lines across to show that, and perhaps color it with crayons.

Artalk Artalk Artalk Artalk Artalk

What rooms do those windows look out of? Is there a garage? Where is it? When you leave for school in the morning, do you usually go out the front door? When you get home from school, is there a person to greet you, or must you open the door with a key? What do you do while you wait for the grownups to return?

WHAT I LIKE TO DO ON SUNDAY AFTERNOON

Encouraging Recollection

You'll Need
White drawing paper 12 in. × 18 in. or 9 in. × 12 in., black thin-line markers, pencils.

Let's Go
Use the Artalk questions only as much as needed to generate

responses. The children may choose the size of paper that suits them best. If they decide to show more than one idea, they may fold their papers in halves or in quarters. As they begin to draw, tell them to keep in mind the details that will make clear to the viewer where the activity is taking place. They should draw themselves first in the appropriate position for the activity, then the objects which would be below, above and next to themselves, and then gradually add details that radiate from the center of interest. Give suggestions for drawing figures who are seated, lying down or facing backwards. The children may use each other as models. They should draw details in clothing as well as such items as watches, glasses, shoelaces, or a patch on blue jeans if the pose shows it. Interior pictures should include furniture, light fixtures, rugs, pictures on the wall, plant stands, bookcases, and so on. Outdoor pictures may include a driveway, garbage cans, clothesline, mailbox, doghouse, or wood pile. If the scene is a public place, street lights, billboards, storefronts, parked or moving cars, fire hydrants, bus stop sign, or outdoor seating can be included. Crowds of people at the movies or in an arena can be implied by little circles or scallops high on the paper.

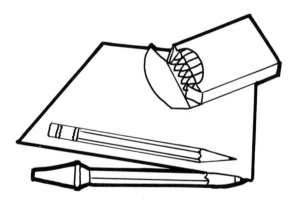

Artalk Artalk Artalk Artalk Artalk

How many of you usually go somewhere on Sunday afternoon? Who goes with parents or friends to someone's house to visit or play games? How many of you visit your grandparents regularly? How many of you have a mother or father who doesn't live at your house? Do you sometimes see each other on Sunday? Where do you like to go together? Do you ever walk your dog on Sunday afternoon or take it to a park or field where it can run? Do some of you usually stay at home on Sunday afternoon? Is there a special program on TV you like to watch? What position do you like when you are watching TV: in a comfortable chair, lying on a couch, nestled in a beanbag, or sprawled on the floor? Do you like to read the comics in the Sunday paper, or read a good book? Do you or your parents ever make popcorn on Sunday afternoon or some other tasty snack?

(As the children are finishing) Who is ready to show their picture? Tell us exactly what's going on in your picture. What time is it in your picture? Is your picture showing what you did *last* Sunday afternoon? When, exactly? Who else is ready to show?

(Teachers and leaders should be alert to responses that may be shared in a matter-of-fact way, but which cover deep feelings. It is wise not to press the children when they seem unable to speak further.)

ON THE PLAYGROUND

Increasing Perception

You'll Need
Manila paper 12 in. × 18 in., crayons or colored markers.

Let's Go
Spend at least ten minutes discussing what games the children play, either at a park, in a neighbor's yard, or on a playground. Ask them to describe any apparatus that may be present such as swings or slides. Ask them to tell you exactly what they see beyond them while they are playing—steps to a house, trees, a garage, the side of a building. Tell them to draw themselves playing a specific game with their friends. Encourage them to recall carefully how things look. If a child needs help with a certain pose, enlist a child to "model" for a few minutes to help clarify the shape. Each child should color brightly. Each person in the picture should be at least as big as the flat of a hand on the paper so that it is possible to put in details of clothing and facial features.

Artalk Artalk Artalk Artalk Artalk

Where are you playing? What game is it? Which one is you? Who are the other children?

LOOKING IN THE WINDOW

Encouraging Observation and Recollection

You'll Need

Gray construction paper 9 in. × 12 in., manila drawing paper 9 in. × 12 in., scissors, white glue, crayons or colored markers, clear plastic wrap cut in pieces 11 in. × 14 in.

Let's Go

Use the Artalk questions first. Tell the children to fold the gray construction paper in half. With the paper folded, they should cut out a "window," leaving about an inch frame around the edge of the paper. The frame by the folded edge should be thinner. The children can now unfold the paper and press it flat. This is the "window with two panes." Now, on the manila paper they should draw what they see in the "window." Encourage details. When the children are finished with their pictures they should turn over the paper and place glue all around the edge. They can then center the paper onto the plastic wrap, and fold the edges of the plastic over the glue and seal them. Presto! Glass in the window! Now they can put glue on the back side of the window frame and glue it on top of the "glass."

fold

6"

9"

PAPER

Artalk Artalk Artalk Artalk Artalk

Who knows what "window shopping" is? Do you like to window shop?
Do you ever window shop with your mother or father or with a friend?
What store windows do you especially like to look in?

Try to remember a special store window. Draw it and color it.
When you are all finished making your picture, cover it with "glass" and
a window frame. Then show us your window and tell us about it.

WHAT I DO WHEN I GET HOME FROM SCHOOL

Encouraging Recollection

You'll Need
Manila drawing paper 12 in. × 18 in. or 9 in. × 12 in., crayons,
pencils, thin-line or standard size colored markers, white chalk, facial
tissue.

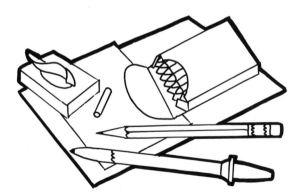

Let's Go

Use the Artalk questions first. The children may choose the size of paper that suits them best. When they begin to draw, they may want to use white chalk to sketch out ideas. They can use facial tissues to wipe out lines they don't want. They should put themselves in the picture first, making sure that the shape of the figure is at least as big as the flat of their hand on the paper. If they draw themselves big, it will be easier to add details to make the picture stories more interesting. If they have difficulty with side poses or seated figures (such as a person seated in front of a TV), show them some simple shapes they can use. They may also ask a friend to pose in positions that are difficult to draw without a model. Some children enjoy using pencils or thin-line markers, which allow them to add intricate details in clothing and environment. Those who make less complex drawings can use their standard size markers or crayons to color basic shapes.

Artalk Artalk Artalk Artalk Artalk

What do you do after school? How many of you ride the school bus home? How many of you are picked up by someone in a car? How many of you walk home? How many of you have some sort of practice after school? Does anyone have music lessons or an after-school activity like Brownies or Cub Scouts? If you go right home, what do you like to do? Play with your friends until suppertime? How many of you have to look after a younger sister or brother? Does anyone have to wait at home until your parents return from work? What do you do while you are waiting? Watch cartoons on TV? Does anyone play video games? Take the dog for a walk? Does anyone have a special job to help get supper started before the grownups come? Picture yourself in a location where you often find yourself after school; draw it and later on we'll talk about it.

(As the children are finishing) Who is ready to show their picture? What are you doing in your picture? Tell us about the details you have included. Is after school a good time for you, or just a so-so time? Can you tell why?

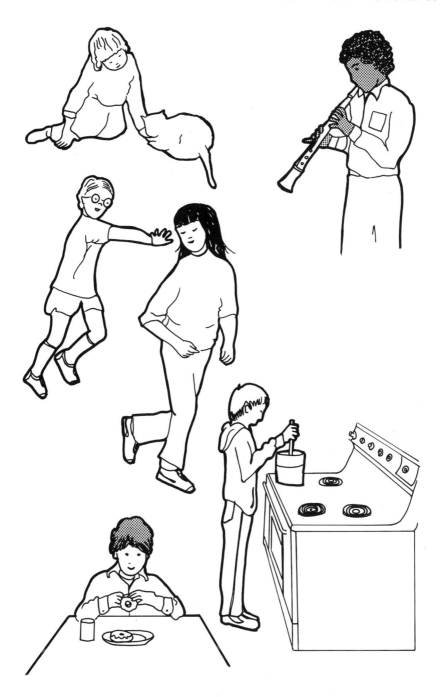

GOING TO WORK

Encouraging Recollection and Attention to Detail

You'll Need
Manila paper 12 in. × 18 in., colored markers or crayons.

Let's Go
Talk to the children about the people at their house who go to work. It could be mother, father, brother, sister, or another relative. They should try to think of one particular person and what that person wears at work, or what their work place looks like. The children might envision lunch boxes, uniforms being washed, briefcases, papers, hard hats, a tool box, or a place they may have visited—an office, a factory, or a construction site. If they have no recollection of a person from home going to work, they might draw a picture of an uncle or aunt or a special adult friend whose work schedule is familiar. Otherwise they can draw persons dressed for and engaged in work about the house.

Encourage the children to draw what they can remember to help them tell something about a place of work or a person going to work. Encourage them to include specific details. The finished drawing may be nothing more than a rough sketch. The picture will be used to support information that will be offered during the Artalk.

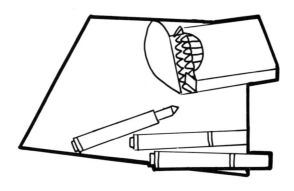

Artalk Artalk Artalk Artalk Artalk

Can you name a place where a person at your house, or another person whom you know goes to work? Does this job require special clothes? Who can try to describe them? How many of the working people whom you know carry their lunch? How? In a lunch box, in a paper sack, or a briefcase? How many of you have visited a place where your father, mother, or another person at your home works? Perhaps you can describe that place in your picture.

(For those children who have chosen to draw home duties.) What kinds of jobs are necessary around the house? Do you sometimes help? Perhaps you can draw someone doing housework or working in the yard.

(As the children finish) Who is ready to show their picture? Tell us about everything in it. Was the picture hard to make? Why?

Note to teachers and leaders: Some children will find it difficult to hide strong feelings as they show these pictures. Accept all responses with equanimity.

MY FAVORITE STORY

Encouraging Fluency and Perception

You'll Need
Colored construction paper (all colors except black) 12 in. × 18 in., oil crayons, 3 in. × 5 in. index cards, pencils, white chalk.

Let's Go
Discuss with the children their favorite stories. Let them tell you the name of a library book they especially like. If they don't go to the library, they may tell about another book they have at home, or about a

story they know. They are to draw pictures of their favorite story, using oil crayons on colored paper. To help them get started, they may sketch the major shapes on the paper with white chalk. If "mistakes" are made with the chalk, they can easily be wiped out and redrawn. Encourage them to draw large and make the most important thing in the picture clear by outlining it with a contrasting color. They should press heavily with their crayons so that their colors show up on the bright paper. Tell them to think of details that will make the pictures more interesting, and a background that is appropriate. This project should be divided into two work periods; it takes time to make the entire space interesting. When finished they may print the name of the story on the 3 in. × 5 in. card with a pencil, and underneath print "illustrated by" and their names.

Artalk Artalk Artalk Artalk Artalk

What did you choose as your favorite story? Why is it your favorite? What scene are you showing in your picture? Tell us more about your story. Perhaps some of the children would like to read it, if they haven't already.

ALL BY MYSELF

Encouraging Recollection

You'll Need
Manila drawing paper 12 in. × 18 in. or 9 in. × 12 in., colored markers, crayons.

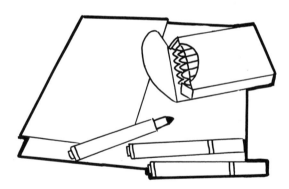

Let's Go
Use the Artalk questions first. Give the children their choice of paper. Their drawings may be nothing but simple sketches to illustrate their explanations. Allow plenty of time for show and tell. There might be a little reluctance at first to show these pictures. It takes just one trusting child to come forth with candid revelations; this sets a tone that will free other children to make candid responses as well. The leader

must be especially sensitive and respectful, whatever the level of personal sharing that ensues. Some children hate being alone, and will vehemently say so. These declarations should be accepted in a matter-of-fact way without undue concern. Their pictures will be adjusted accordingly (see Artalk).

Artalk Artalk Artalk Artalk Artalk

How many of you like to be alone sometimes? Where do you like to be alone? Did you ever climb a tree? Is it fun to sit above everything and

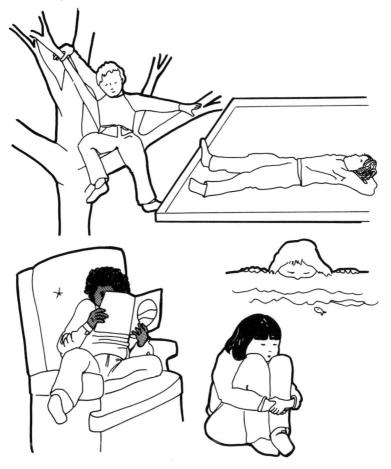

look around you? Did you ever lie on your back or on a flat roof and watch the clouds go by? Or at night gaze up at the stars? Did you ever lie on your stomach looking down into a deep pool of water and perhaps drop pebbles to watch the water ripple? A lot of grownups like to fish by themselves. Have any of you tried it? In your house, what do you like to do when no one else is around? Do you like to sing or draw pictures? Who likes to read or look at books? How many of you have a pet? Is it small enough to hold? Do you like to hold your pet and talk to it? Or do you like to sit by yourself in a special hideaway and think or daydream? What are some of your best dreams? As soon as you have an idea of what you'd like to draw, you may begin.

(For those who don't like to be alone) Draw someone else in the picture with you.

WHAT I DO WHEN I GET UP IN THE MORNING

Encouraging Recollection

You'll Need
White drawing paper 12 in. × 18 in., crayons, colored thin-line markers, pencils (optional).

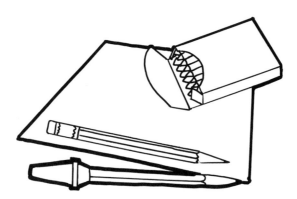

Let's Go

Discuss with the children their daily routine. Encourage them to visualize their various morning duties—walking the dog, helping to make breakfast, brushing their teeth, waking up a younger sister, and so on. Try to personalize this as much as possible. The more specific the children are in their descriptions, the more detail will appear in their pictures. After the children have listened to each other, tell them to pick a scene from their morning routine and draw it as carefully as they can. They may start with pencil if they choose, then go over the pencil with marker. They may color in areas if they wish but entreat them to color *carefully* so they don't destroy details.

Artalk Artalk Artalk Artalk Artalk

Show us what you are doing. What room are you in? What time is it? Tell us what all the objects are in your picture.

EATING OUT

Encouraging Personal Expression

You'll Need
Manila drawing paper or newsprint 12 in. × 18 in. for each child, crayons, pencils, or felt-tip markers.

Let's Go
Use the questions below or substitute more specific questions according to the class. Show examples of people turned away, seated in chairs. Show how the table fits on each side of the body. Show how the people at the end of the table look like stairsteps. Show how people across the table seem "cut off" because the table is in front of them. Encourage the children to draw as many details as they can remember. Be sure that they draw themselves and the people they eat with.

Artalk Artalk Artalk Artalk Artalk

Does your family ever eat out? Where do they go? What is the name of the place? Describe the inside. Are there windows? Are there fancy light fixtures? Do you sit in a booth or at a table? Is it round or square or rectangular? Are there waitresses or waiters? What do they wear? Does Mom or Dad go up to the counter to get the order? Are there signs advertising the food they sell? Is there a counter where some people sit?

WHAT I WANT TO BE
WHEN I GROW UP

Encouraging Perception and Recall

You'll Need

Colored construction paper 6 in. × 18 in., oil crayons, white chalk.

Let's Go

Use the Artalk questions first. Tell the children that when they begin to draw, they should divide the space on the paper in three general areas for the head, body, and legs. They can start by making a large oval which should be placed about two inches from the top of the paper. This will allow space for a hat or a cap if there is one on the head. Add a neck at the bottom of the head; this will connect with a rectangle representing the body form. The bottom of this rectangle should fall at about the center of the paper. The lower space will be devoted to legs and feet. These first outlines can be sketched in with white chalk which can be erased easily with a sweep of the hand.

Clothing often identifies a person's occupation. The children may have difficulty drawing appropriate hats or collars. Try to find a cap with a visor in front to show the children who want to draw a pilot, a person in the armed services, or one in police work. Some children may want help with a cowboy hat, and how it sits on a head.

Feet and hands need special attention as well. Ask a child to stand on a stool so that the others can see that when a person is facing them, the sides of the feet don't show. An open hand or a hand holding something can be simplified to a few basic lines. The children can ask each other to model hand positions if necessary. It would be helpful if the leader or teacher could outline some of these different shapes on a chalkboard or a large sheet of paper taped to a wall. When the children

are ready to start filling in their drawings, urge them to press hard with their oil crayons so that the colors show up on the colored paper. They should use the appropriate skin color for face and hands (peach or brown).

Artalk Artalk Artalk Artalk Artalk

Ask "What do you want to be when you grow up?" As the children answer, write their responses on the chalkboard or a large piece of paper tacked to a wall. When it seems that most of the children have responded, go back to the first response on the list and ask "What does a _____ wear? What might a _____ carry in hand?" Go down the list, repeating these same questions. Then say to the children, "Try to show us by the clothes you put on your figure, by the object carried, or by a background clue, what you'd like to be. When you have finished, we will take turns looking at the results and identifying the things that show the occupation of the person you have drawn."

PHOTO ALBUM

Stimulating Recall and Perception

You'll Need
Newsprint or white drawing paper 3 in. $\times$ 18 in., thin-line markers or pencils.

Let's Go
Tell the children to fold the long strip of paper in half, then in half again the same way. They should take care that the corners meet. Then they may fold the paper one more time in the same direction.

When the paper is unfolded to its full length there should be eight rectangles. Now the children should refold the paper on the same folds, back and forth to create accordion pleats. They should draw a line on each crease to separate the sections. The children are to pretend that they are going on a trip to a foreign land and they have room in their luggage to take along just eight photos of family and friends. They are to use their marker or pencil to draw the persons, pets, or objects that they want to remember and keep with them. Challenge the children to try to draw a special feature which would help to identify each person— dark hair, glasses, a long neck, a chubby face, a special dress or shirt that a certain person often wears. They may include their pets or a particular place that they want to remember. Assure them that their drawings aren't expected to be likenesses, but the exercise is giving them a chance to think of special visual features of each choice.

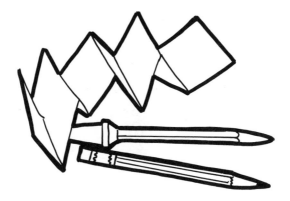

Artalk Artalk Artalk Artalk Artalk

Do you know someone who has a wallet with pictures in it? Has anyone ever seen a wallet that has a photo folder in it? They fold back and forth just like your paper. How many of you are going to choose members of your family for your photo folder? Does anyone have a grandma or grandpa who is going to appear in your folder? Who has a special aunt, uncle, or cousin you want to add? How many of you have a special friend you are going to put in your album? Pets? Who has a special place they want to include in their album? (When the children are finished, they may share their albums in small groups of three or four, show their pictures to each other, and tell about them.)

WHERE I'D RATHER BE

Encouraging Recollection and/or Imagination

You'll Need

Manila paper 12 in. × 18 in., colored chalk or markers, white chalk, newsprint 9 in. × 12 in., charcoal fixative or hair spray, facial tissues.

Let's Go

Pick a day when the children can't play outside because of rain or cold.

Tell the children that they can transport themselves anywhere, using their imagination. Tell them to close their eyes and concentrate on a place they would rather be. They can pick any location, real or imaginary. Use the Artalk questions before continuing.

Tell the children to use the white chalk to sketch on the paper the main divisions of the picture: sky, water, mountains, flat land, major shapes. Then, starting at the upper half of the picture (if using chalk) they can begin to tone in their ideas, using the side of the chalk, and pressing lightly at first. If they use markers, they should sketch first, using short strokes.* If they continue using chalk, they should lay

---

*If chalk and markers are both used, it is best to use the markers first, as the chalk will clog the felt tip.

newsprint under their hand to avoid smears. Tell them that a chalk picture usually looks soft and the edges of things blurry, so they should not worry about details. They may use tissues to blend the colors. Dark outlines distinguishing specific shapes should not be added until near the end of their work.

Artalk Artalk Artalk Artalk Artalk

If you could be anywhere in the world today, where would you rather be? Shut your eyes, and when you have an idea, raise your hand and describe the place as carefully as you can. Would you like to be where it's warm? What would be in a picture that would make it look *warm*? Who would like to be on a tropical island? What might you see there? Who wants to be at the seashore? What can you put in your picture to make it interesting? Who wants to go to outer space? What will you put in your picture? Who would rather be at home playing with your friends, or visiting with Grandma? Think of what you will need to include in your picture to show us where it is. When you are finished we want to see your pictures and have you tell us where you'd rather be.

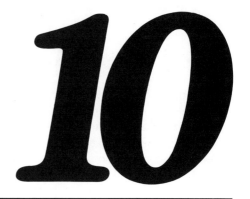

TELL ME
ABOUT THINGS
YOU DISCOVERED

Little children pay more attention to lines, colors, shapes, and textures than many adults do. Standing in front of an abstract painting in an art museum, an adult may be speechless, while a child, transfixed, gasps, "Oh, how neat!" Children intuitively recognize aesthetic quality. They are captivated by the drama of two colors merging together, or by the graceful swirl of fingerpaint. They are entranced by the feel of cool, smooth marble, or by the complexity of an intricately woven fabric. With the battery of sights and sounds inherent in today's ever-present media, children can grow insensitive to these simple pleasures. Thus it becomes an important mission for an adult to present to the children these aesthetic wonders as single encounters to enjoy and savor, one by one.

A teacher can easily persuade children to ease off from their typically frenzied activity for the purpose of looking at and comparing elements in art—lines, shapes, colors, values, or textures. Teachers or leaders, sure that the aim of art is only to make something, need to be reminded that the act of making involves choosing and discarding as well as observing. The making includes the false starts, the happy accidents, the carefully designed discoveries, as well. All of these experiences provide memorable learning. In a relaxed atmosphere, the process of looking and comparing, as well as doing makes children eager to talk. An enthusiastic teacher, inspired by the involvement of the children in these sensory delights, will stir the children to talk all the more.

LEARNING TO LOOK

Increasing Perceptual Awareness

You'll Need
White drawing paper 9 in. × 18 in., scissors, crayons, a copy of *Look Again* by Tana Hoban (New York: Macmillan, 1971).

Let's Go
Tell the children that art is created by *looking, thinking,* and *choosing.*

Gather the children into a circle near you. Read *Look Again* to them, letting them guess what is behind every "hole." Tell the children that artists like to study details of things around them; when they draw or paint their pictures, they add details to make them more interesting. Each child is to fold the paper in *half.* In the top half a small hole should be cut near the middle. (Some children will need assistance with this.) Ask each of the children to make a picture on the bottom half, and draw in details carefully so that when the "peek-a-boo" page is folded over the picture, the viewer will have an interesting detail to look at and will want to see more.

Artalk Artalk Artalk Artalk Artalk

Show your picture and call on your friends to guess what's inside the "hole." When someone has guessed right, show us your entire picture and tell us more about it. How did you think of this idea?

DANCING CLOWNS

Exploring Movement and Proportion

You'll Need

Paste, crayons, scissors, colored scrap paper, one piece of peach or brown construction paper 2 in. × 3 in. (head), one piece of construction paper any color 3 in. × 5 in. (body), two pieces of construction paper any color 1 in. × 8 in. (legs), two pieces of construction paper any color 1 in. × 6 in. (arms).

Let's Go

Pass out the six pieces of construction paper to each child. Tell the children that the pieces are part of a puzzle they must solve. They are to construct a human figure from the pieces. They will probably identify the parts and assemble them quickly. The result will be a figure with straight arms and legs. Now ask the children if they can make the figure run or jump. Call a volunteer to pose stiff-legged, stiff-armed. Now ask the volunteer to pretend to be running or catching a ball. What bends? Elbows and knees. Some will suggest cutting or folding the arm and leg pieces. Tell the children to cut the arm and leg pieces in half and reassemble the figure so that it is jumping or running. Remind the children that arms stick out of the top of the body. (Some will insist on inserting the arms in the middle.) Tell the children to experiment with several action poses. Once they have decided on one they like, they should paste all their pieces together. After the Artalk questions, the children should add clown details.

Artalk Artalk Artalk Artalk Artalk

Where have you seen a clown? In a supermarket, in a parade, or on TV? Who has seen a *real* clown at a circus? Can you describe a clown costume? What do clowns have on their faces? What do clowns do? (Somersault, juggle, run, flirt, shake hands with little babies). What can you add to the figure to make it look like a clown? Use scrap paper to add pointed hats, stand-up hair, big ears, big buttons or funny shoes.

(As the children are finishing) Who is ready to show their clown? Was it fun to put your clown together? Was it hard to make it look "right?" Where did you get the idea for the clown costume? Can you pose in the same position as your clown?

FITTING A BODY INTO A PRE-CUT SHAPE

Stimulating Awareness of Body Shapes

You'll Need
Colored construction paper 12 in. × 18 in. cut into large shapes such as circles, half circles, squares, rectangles, triangles, trapezoids, and simple letter shapes (S, T, X, C, V), oil crayons.

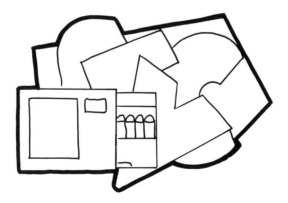

Let's Go

Tell the children that the human body can bend and curve to make almost any shape. Hold up one of the geometric shapes. Ask a volunteer to pose in a position that would fill the shape you are holding. Hold up one more and call one more volunteer before you distribute the paper shapes. Tell the children to think hard before they decide what to make. Encourage them to "try out" their shape by asking a friend to pose, or to go to a full-length mirror, if you have one, where they can study the pose. Then they should make the figure in the shape they have been given. Tell the children to think of a particular time when a person would be in that position. Have them dress the person accordingly and add background details showing where the person is. Tell them to press hard with the oil crayon to create a nice contrast with the colored paper.

Artalk Artalk Artalk Artalk Artalk

What kind of a person did you make? What time of day is it? Where is the person? Pose in the same position you have drawn. Was it pretty hard to draw your person so it looked right? Are you satisfied with your drawing? What could make it better?

IMAGINARY ANIMALS

Discovering the Possibilities in Torn Paper

You'll Need
1 piece plain or colored newsprint 9 in. × 12 in. and 18 in. × 24 in. for each child, colored markers, paste or glue.

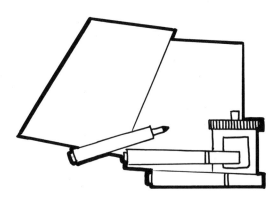

Let's Go

Tell the children that it's fun to rip paper, and that they can make all kinds of objects, animals, and people this way. Use the Artalk discussion before you continue. A rip down the short side of the large paper will quickly produce a tail for an animal. The rip may produce a long or a short tail. Tearing is always an adventure! You're never sure what path the tear will take. The children can control the direction somewhat by moving both hands along both sides of the tear as they are ripping the paper.

To make the legs of the animal they can tear a "door" out of the bottom of the paper. This "door" can be used for the head. What's left over represents the legs. Tell the children that tearing paper produces no mistakes, only unexpected results. Urge the children to continue to tear freely; they can add to the shapes that need to be expanded simply by pasting more torn pieces in appropriate places. Tearing evokes a spirit of play, and as the children relax and start to have fun, they will start naming each piece that they tear off. "This looks like a . . . ." If you challenge them, some will discover how to make the animal's eye by folding and tearing the paper.

The children can use markers to make details—bumps, claws, hair, saddles, noses, teeth, and so on. A blank wall (perhaps a long hall) would be a perfect display area for a "parade of animals."

Artalk Artalk Artalk Artalk Artalk

How many of you remember when you were really little and you liked to rip paper? Did you ever get a chance to do it? Ripping makes a great sound, and you can make amazing things with ripped paper. Let's everyone, without looking, rip one shape out of the small paper and say what it looks like. Now we'll make imaginary animals. When you are finished you must give the animal a name. The animal may be very floppy, but we can tape it to the wall in several places and then you can tell us all about it.

(After the animals are taped to a wall) Who wants to tell about their animal? What was the name you decided on? Do you think tearing an animal is more fun than cutting one out? If you had drawn the animal first, do you think it would be as interesting?

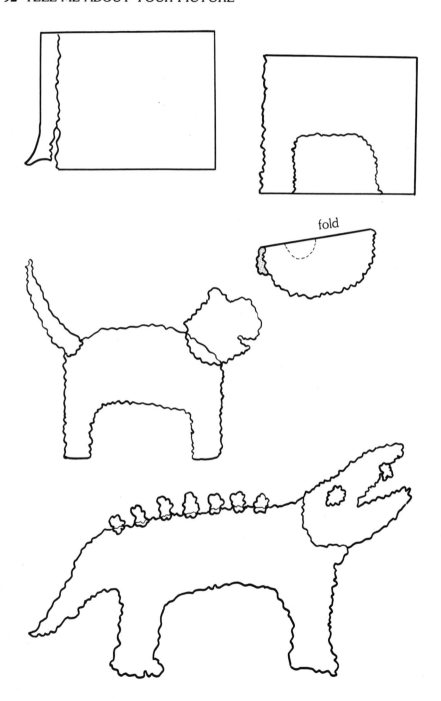

fold

CLAY TILES

Discovering Pattern in Texture

You'll Need

Moist clay (about the size of a baseball) for each child, newsprint 9 in. × 12 in., an assortment of objects that may be pressed into clay to make interesting textures (such as bottle caps, paper clips, wooden dowels, potato mashers, tongue depressors, scissors, forks, clay tools, a table knife), a rolling pin covered with cheesecloth for every five children. (If rolling pins aren't available, the sides of a stiff cardboard tube, or a can or jar wrapped in cloth, can be used to roll out the clay.)

Let's Go

Tell the children to roll the clay flat on the newsprint. Tell them the slab should be at least as thick as their middle finger. Let the children experiment making impressions with the objects at their tables. Let them freely exchange objects and comments. Encourage them to try repeating an impression of one object several times for an interesting texture.

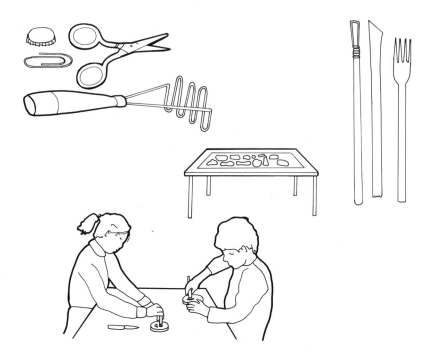

After an ample discovery period (about ten minutes), tell the children they will have to decide on the combination of textures they want to keep. They may gather the clay into a ball and roll it out once more. This time they should be more selective with the objects and placement of impressions. Use the knife to cut the outside form into a pleasing shape. Tell them that if they cannot pick the clay up easily it is too big or too thin, so they will have to make adjustments accordingly. Wad the rest of the clay into a ball and place it in an airtight container for future use.

Lay a piece of white or colored paper on a large table. Have the children, one at a time, place their slabs in relationship to one another on the colored paper so that the clay tiles look nice together. Encourage some of the children to leave empty spaces so that the colored paper shows through. After all the tiles are arranged into one design, let the class gather around the table and comment on them. (Use the Artalk questions now.)

Store the clay tiles carefully until they are bone dry. If you have access to a kiln, bisque-fire the pieces. Be sure to explain to the children that the firing process will change the color of the tiles but will make them much more permanent.

Artalk Artalk Artalk Artalk Artalk

Which of the tiles do you like best? Which shape makes a nice pattern when it is repeated over and over? Tell us about the objects you used to make your design. Why did you choose that particular combination of objects? Did you discover that combination right away or after you had experimented for awhile?

Do you like working with clay? What makes working with clay so great? (For dissenters) Why don't you like working with clay?

*BIRD PATTERNS**

Seeing Negative Shapes

You'll Need
Tagboard square 3 in. × 3 in., light-colored construction paper 12 in. × 18 in., oil crayons, scissors, pencil

Let's Go
Use the Artalk questions first. Tell each child to make a bird shape that touches at least three sides of the tagboard square. Legs or

---

*Idea first published in *Arts and Activities* (Vol. 88, No. 1, p. 4950), "Birds, a Vehicle for Design" by Janet Carson. San Diego, CA, September 1980.

feet must be thick enough to be cut out with scissors. The bird may be flying, nesting or perching. Now they are to cut out the bird shape and trace it over and over, in four rows, on the large paper. The resulting pattern can be colored with oil crayons both inside and out; other shapes may have been created in the empty spaces. When they color their designs, they can make colored lines as well as shapes, and add decorative detail in the empty spaces as well as eyes or wings within the bird form. Urge the children to select colors that will look nice with the background color and to use them consistently throughout to make a unified design.

Artalk Artalk Artalk Artalk Artalk

What kinds of birds can you name? Do any of you or your friends feed the birds? Did you ever see ducks in a pond? Are they birds, too? Who knows an easy way to make a bird shape? (Let one child draw a shape on a chalkboard or on a piece of paper where all the children can see.) Can anyone else come and draw another shape? We are going to use bird shapes to make an interesting pattern.

(After the lesson is completed) What kind of bird did you use for your pattern? Show us how you decorated the empty spaces.

*SHIVER PICTURES**

Encouraging Creative Expression

You'll Need

Variety of bright colors of construction paper 9 in. × 12 in., box of crayons, paste or glue, 1 piece of 3 in. × 4 in. pink or tan construction paper for each child, colored paper scraps.

---

*Idea first published in *School Arts* (Vol. 80, No. 2, pp. 15–16), "Design: Torn Paper" by Janet Carson. Baton Rouge, LA, October 1980.

Let's Go

Pick a cold day for this activity.* Put on a hat, scarf and mittens. The children will be mystified! Ask the children to stand up and *shiver*. The teacher might then ask: "What do you do with your hands when you shiver? Hug yourself? Press your arms to your sides? Let's make a shiver by tearing paper." It's hard to do, but the torn edges will look as though they are shivering. Start with the pink or tan paper for the head. Make it big. Then tear out pieces for eyes, mouth, red cheeks, hair, cap or hat. Maybe earmuffs! Turn the colored paper the short or long way for the size coat and pants you want. Mittens are easy—just tear a circle and take a little bite out of it. Remember, when you hug yourself, your thumbs are up. Don't forget your scarf or your shoes!

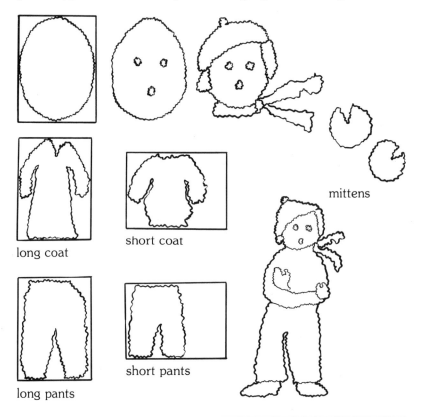

mittens

long coat

short coat

long pants

short pants

---

*If the climate in your area is always warm, switch to "after swimming" or "being caught without a raincoat in the rain." Clothing will change to bathing suits, shirts, and pants accordingly.

Artalk Artalk Artalk Artalk Artalk

Tell us about a time when you really got cold. Where was it? What did you do?

FANTASTIC CREATURES

Discovering Found Shapes to Make New Forms

You'll Need
Magazines, assorted colors of construction paper 12 in. × 18 in., scissors, paste or white glue.

Let's Go
Tell the children that it is fun to look at common shapes and think of them in a new way. A famous artist, Pablo Picasso, did this when he looked at a bicycle seat and decided that it looked like a bull's head. The handlebars reminded him of a bull's horns, so he put them together to make an amusing sculpture. Tell the children to look through magazines for shapes that remind them of parts of a bird, fish,

or creature. (Use the Artalk questions now.) After the discussion they can assemble the shapes that remind them of body parts. These can be put together into a fantastic montage. They should choose the color of background paper that will contrast best with the pieces they have cut out.

Artalk Artalk Artalk Artalk Artalk

If you were looking for parts of a bird, a fish, or some sort of creature, what would round shapes remind you of? (Eyes, hands, bodies.) What would long, skinny shapes remind you of? (Neck, legs, trunks, bodies.) What about soft, fluffy shapes? (Tails, fins, feathers.)

(When the lesson is completed) Where did you find the pieces for your picture? Was it hard to find the pieces you needed to add to those you started with? Did you think this was fun, or would you rather *draw* a fantastic creature? Do you think you could make up one as good as the one you have made with the magazine cutouts?

Who has thought of a name for their creature? Where does it live? What does it eat? What kind of a noise does it make? Do you see another one which has been created here today who might be a good companion for the one you made? Why do you think they might be pals?

TEXTURE DESIGN

Discovering Texture with Rubbings

You'll Need
Unwrapped crayons, white or colored newsprint 12 in. × 18 in., pastel construction paper 12 in. × 18 in., scissors, white glue or paste.

Let's Go
Ask the children if any of them have ever put a piece of paper over a penny or a nickel and used their pencils to shade over the bumps made by the coins underneath. The shape of the coin comes through, even the design and the words that are on the coin. The result is called a rubbing. Many artists use rubbings in their work. Lay a piece of newsprint on a textured wall or any surface that has a texture that will be visible to the children. Using the side of a crayon, show the children how to press gently so that the texture of the surface comes through. Each child may now take a piece of newsprint and an unwrapped crayon and look for good surface textures around the room that might make good rubbings. As the children find good textures, they should make rubbings of them on their newsprint. If they fill one sheet, they can take another, and change colors of crayon whenever they wish. Good rubbings can be made on brick, electrical outlets, air vents, key holes and over raised letters on signs. The children might look for books with

raised letters, or embossed leather belts to make interesting rubbings. For another idea, suggest that they look on the bottoms of their shoes. When the excitement of discovery seems to lull, ask the children to sit down and look at the rubbings they have made. They should cut around their best rubbings and arrange them into a design or a picture on the background paper of their choice. When they have decided on the placement of their pieces, they should use paste sparingly to attach them to the background paper or it will show through the thin newsprint.

Artalk Artalk Artalk Artalk Artalk

Where did you find your best textures? What's fun about making texture rubbings? Do your rubbings look as good as they felt? Who was surprised by a texture that made a better rubbing than they thought it would? Any disappointments?

TEXTURE MONTAGE

Discovering That
Repeated Textures Make Patterns

You'll Need
Colored construction paper 9 in. × 12 in. and 12 in. × 18 in., a magazine for each child (magazines should have colored photographs, as do *National Geographic*, *Better Homes and Gardens*, *Modern Maturity*), scissors, white glue or paste.

Let's Go
Tell the children to look through their magazines for textures that make repeated patterns. Some examples might be:

- fluted sides of cabinets
- velour seat covers (car)
- grainy texture of luggage
- windows on a skyscraper
- bricks on a patio
- blades of grass

As the children find these patterns, they are to cut them out. They might have to slice right through a picture to get the pieces they

want. After they have cut a sizable batch, they should spread them out and decide how to assemble them into a montage. A montage is a picture made with pieces of other pictures or designs from newspapers or magazines. They should choose a color of background paper that will complement the texture patterns. Suggest that the size of background paper that they choose might depend on the number and/or size of the pieces they have gathered. It might be nice to simply overlap the pieces into an interesting cluster of colored patterns. If they choose to cut their pieces into uniform shapes such as in diamonds, or squares, these can be assembled like a patchwork quilt. Another idea would be to cut the pieces in interlocking shapes like a puzzle. To make a balanced design, they can start pasting pieces in the middle of their background paper and add pieces that radiate out from there, or they can paste their patterns in rows. They might like to let the background paper peek through. Their designs will look more finished if they leave a space around the outside edges for a border. Remind the children to use their paste sparingly so that it won't leak out.

Artalk Artalk Artalk Artalk Artalk

Tell us where you found your textures. What kind of a design did you decide to make? Which pattern do you like best? Which patterns look nice side by side?

LINES OF PEOPLE

Learning to Overlap

You'll Need
White drawing paper 12 in. × 18 in., six pieces of light-colored Fadeless® paper 4½ in. × 9 in. for each child, pencil, black thin-line markers, scissors, white glue or paste.

Let's Go
Enlist the help of four volunteers. Tell two of them to stand in front of the rest of the children. The other two should stand behind the first two. Tell the children to notice that the two children in back are only partially seen. The bodies of the children in front overlap the bodies of the children standing behind them. After the volunteers are seated, tell the children to draw the outline of a person on the white side of one of their small pieces of Fadeless® paper. The drawing can be very simple,

but must be as big as their paper. They might think of a gingerbread man cookie shape as they make their drawing. Move around among the children and tell those who are drawing too small to redraw it bigger on the same sheet. (The redrawn sketch won't show because it will be on the back of the finished picture.) After they have made their drawing big enough, the children should gather all their colored papers together and cut six figures at once, using their drawing as a pattern. Then they may trade with neighbors nearby. They should paste the first three in a line leaving a little space between each figure. Then they should paste the other three figures so that the bodies overlap parts of the first three, just as they observed in the demonstration. The children may use thin-line markers to draw details of clothing and facial features. If they wish, they can try to draw more people standing behind the second row. A good way is to draw scallops or little circles to imply a crowd in the distance. The children should think of an environment for their "crowd" and add appropriate clues, such as signs, buildings, stadium seats, grandstand, spotlights (depending on the story in the picture).

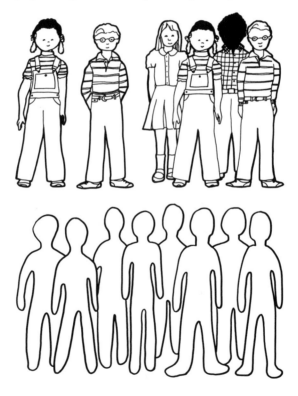

Artalk Artalk Artalk Artalk Artalk

Where do people stand in line, or huddle together, some in back of others? Describe the specific place where your crowd is located. Introduce us to some of the people you have included in your picture.

GANGLING GOBLINS

Creating the Illusion of Movement

You'll Need
Black construction paper 6 in. × 9 in., small pieces of yellow or orange crepe paper, scissors, glue or paste.

Let's Go
At Halloween time it is interesting to make images that are different from the usual black cats, pumpkins and witches. A gangling creature is fun to draw. Show the children a basic skeletal form on a chalkboard or on a piece of paper tacked to a wall. Let them see how the spinal column and the set of shoulders help to determine the posture of the figure. Encourage the children to make the contour of their goblin as

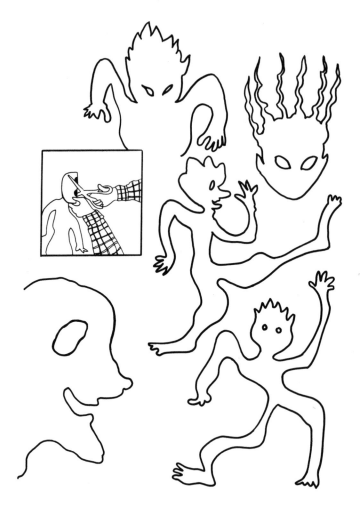

detailed as they can—wild hair, warty nose, toothless smile (if profile view), long nails, hunched shoulders, curled toes. Arms and legs can be elongated and crazily distorted. Tell the children that they should draw so that the top of the hair on the head, the tips of the fingers and toes touch the edges of their black paper. This will assure you that the finished drawings will be big enough for easy cutting. Tell the children to cut slowly, concentrating on one section at a time. Details may be so intricate that they will need to cut little wedges or chunks in order to get into small places. (Be sure that the children have scissors that *cut*.) Control is easier if they open the scissors wide and force the paper between the blades as far as possible. They should turn the paper, not the scissors. To cut out eyes, simply show the students (or let them show you) how to fold the top of the head down and snip out two little "bites." When they have unfolded the paper, they can glue a piece of the crepe paper across the holes on the back of the head.

Artalk Artalk Artalk Artalk Artalk

Does anyone know what distortion means? Who can make a distorted face? How about contortion? Some acrobats can contort their bodies to make amazing shapes. Can any of you do the splits? Who can do a backbend? Who has seen a contortionist at the circus or on TV? You are going to draw a weirdly contorted creature which we'll call a gangling goblin. Pretend that the arms and legs are made of rubber and can do anything. When the goblin is put in the window, orange and yellow eyes will gleam while you tell us which parts of the body you contorted in the goblin you made.

MAKING SLIDES

Discovering Shapes and Textures

You'll Need
A slide projector and a screen, one glass slide mount* for each child, small pieces of blue, yellow and pink cellophane, toothpicks.

Let's Go
Tell the children that artists practice looking very closely at things around them. They get ideas for their art from observing carefully and then recreating familiar images in new ways. Ask the

---

*Available at a photography shop; the slides may be reused.

children if they have ever studied very tiny things through a magnifying glass or a microscope. A drop of water or a fluff of fabric from the inside of a pocket can look very different if magnified many times. When color is added, these can look beautiful. Now the children may open their slides very carefully. If they need help, assist them. They are going to prepare a beautiful slide that will be placed in a projector. They may lay two colors of cellophane in their slide, using a toothpick to overlap them, to make a third color. Now they should reach into their pockets or look around the room for some tiny shapes. Even a piece of thread, a bit of dust, a tiny piece of facial tissue, or crystals of salt or sugar might be interesting when projected on the screen. They can use the toothpick again to push the shapes side by side. If there are empty spaces between, these will create nice shapes, too, when projected. Now they should close their slides firmly. (When placing a slide in the projector, ask the child which side should face up. Place the slide upside down and backwards in the projector so that the image will be projected correctly).

Artalk Artalk Artalk Artalk Artalk

What did you put in your slide? Where did you find your objects? Does your slide remind you of anything you have seen before?

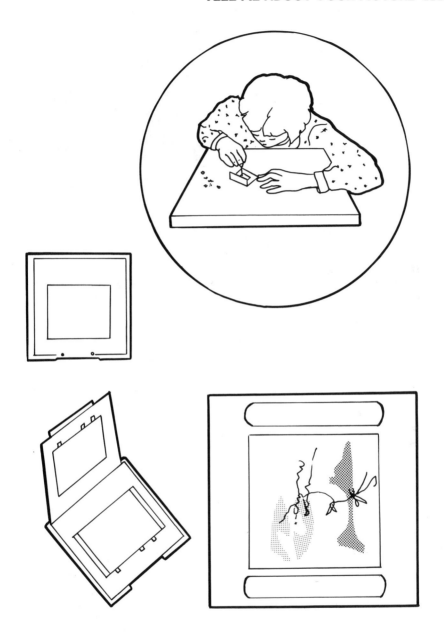

TELL ME ABOUT THINGS YOU LEARNED TO DRAW AND MAKE

Some children like to draw and make things, and if provided with an appropriate setting and art materials, will chart their own course without outside suggestion or stimulation. To them, making pictures or building things are helpful avenues for self-expression. A child can become so involved in an activity that he or she becomes insulated from distractions or comments from others.

With many children, however, this is not the case. Making things in art can pose a threat because of fear of failure or ridicule from friends. A teacher who indulgently urges her flock to "make anything you want" may be disappointed when this "freedom" results in a dead-end. The teacher may be inclined to exclaim, "My kids don't like art!" or "My kids just aren't creative!" The lament "I don't know what to make" may be interpreted as a lack of cooperative spirit or a ploy to gain attention. And yet, many children may truly need guidance and welcome instruction.

Specific art teaching provides children with new knowledge of media and techniques to express their ideas. As children learn and succeed, they become eager to learn more, and their respect for what they are able to do grows.

Even a small success can trigger enthusiasm to try harder, to attend to the task longer, to listen, look, and consider more carefully. The heady sense of accomplishment that results leads to a desire to show and share.

Mastery of art techniques produces exclamations such as "Wait till my brother sees this!" or "This is the best picture I ever made!" or, in open admiration of another, "Gee, Ted, that really looks *neat!*" or "Wow, does that ever look *good!*"

DRAWING MY FRIENDS IN A CIRCLE

Increasing Visual Perception

You'll Need
Manila drawing paper 12 in. × 18 in., broken unwrapped crayons.

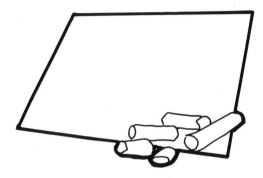

Let's Go
Divide the group in half. Let one group observe the other group standing in a circle holding hands. Tell the observers to notice how their friends look in back as well as how they look in front. Switch groups and let the second group make a circle while the other children watch. Tell all the children to take skin-colored crayons and make five ovals in a row near the top of their papers. These ovals should be spread about two inches apart and be at least an inch high. (It would be helpful if you would demonstrate the size and placement on a piece of paper the same size as theirs.) These will be the faces of their friends; the center oval will be their own. They are to color each face solid and mark over the skin with appropriate colors to make simple features and hair. Then they should pick out one color to make each body and quickly fill it with heavy strokes. Demonstrate how easy it is to use the crayon to make simple shapes and masses. They can make hands and feet with simple knobs on the ends of arms and legs. At the lower middle of the page they can add five more ovals. These will be children with their backs turned, facing the first five. Each oval will be filled with the color of hair. Then

they can quickly crayon in a clothes color for bodies, arms and legs. Encourage the children to omit details. Let them decide how to connect the hands of the children in the back to those of the children in the front. Some of the children may want to know how to draw a side view; help by drawing examples.

Artalk Artalk Artalk Artalk Artalk

Which one is you? What colors have you used that match the clothing you have on? What are the names of the children in the circle? Show us how you have tried to use colors that will remind us of each person.

A BUG IN A RUG

Learning About Design

You'll Need

Colored construction paper 9 in. × 12 in. and 6 in. × 9 in., scissors, white glue or paste, crayons, colored construction paper scraps.

Let's Go

Print the following jingle on a chalkboard or on a large sheet of newsprint and attach it to a wall where the children can see it:

There was a bug
who lived in a rug.
He was a snug
little bug
in a rug.

Ask the children which one of them would like to read the jingle aloud. If there are several volunteers, call on them one after another. Tell the children that before they make their bugs they are going to make rugs with beautiful designs. The design will be balanced, that is, the same on both sides. First of all, they can choose a color that they like for the rug (9 in. × 12 in.), and then another color (6 in. × 9 in.) that will look nice with the first choice. They can cut a fringe on both of the shorter sides of the "rug." To make the design, they should cut narrow strips off of the long sides of the smaller paper. Then they can take the piece that is left and fold it in half the short way. Show them how to cut a diamond on the fold. If they fold the paper twice there will be two diamonds (*if* they are careful to cut the side that has two folds). They should paste the piece that they cut the diamonds out of in the center of the rug. The sides should fit exactly, and the spaces on top and on bottom should be the same, for a formally balanced design. The small strips can be pasted near the fringe edge at each end. The diamond pieces that were cut out can be unfolded, flattened, and pasted in the center or on each side of the middle. Then the children can decorate their rug with crayons, adding more lines across, or drawing

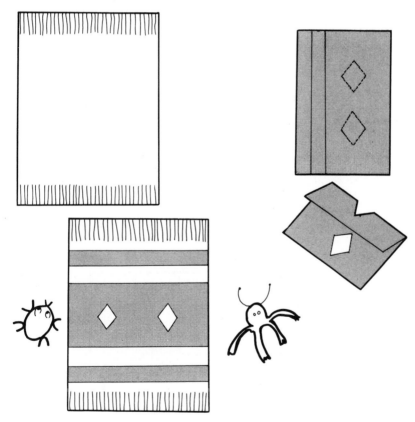

borders around or inside the diamonds. After they have finished the beautiful rug, they can make a bug with colored scraps of paper and attach it permanently with paste, or fasten it on the edge of the rug with a paper clip so that it can be removed to hop around with the aid of its owner.

Artalk Artalk Artalk Artalk Artalk

Show us how you made your balanced design. Is there any special reason why you chose the colors you did for your rug and for the decoration? What kind of bug have you made? Does it have a name? Is he asleep or does he like to hop? Does he do tricks? Show us! Who would like to recite the poem from memory while your bug performs for us?

DRAWING A RABBIT

Encouraging Observation

You'll Need

Gray construction paper 12 in. × 18 in., white chalk, pink oil crayon, black wax crayon, facial tissue, live white rabbit in a cage, fixative.

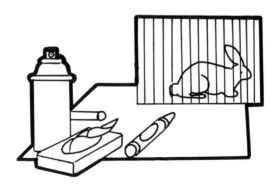

Let's Go

Use the Artalk questions first. Place the rabbit (in its cage) on the floor or table and seat the children so they are facing its sides. A rabbit makes a good model because around strangers it usually freezes motionless; the children can then observe how it looks. Demonstrate with chalk on a piece of the grey construction paper how to block out the major shapes of the body, head, and ears. As the children begin, urge them to draw their basic shapes as large as you have, so the shapes fill the paper. If they want to correct a line, it is easy to wipe off the chalk with a hand and try again. Once they have the form, they should use their black crayon to outline the eyes, whiskers and haunches. Their pink oil crayon can be used to fill in the ears, eyes and nose. Then they can use their white chalk for the body, head, and ears. They may want to smooth out the white chalk with a facial tissue to make the rabbit look fluffy. As they fill in areas with white chalk, urge them to fill in from the top down to avoid accidentally smearing the chalk on the background paper. When the pictures are finished, spray them with charcoal fixative if it is available, or hair spray.

Artalk Artalk Artalk Artalk Artalk

Do you know anyone who has a pet rabbit? Where have you seen a live rabbit before today? As you look at our rabbit, what lines or shapes do you notice especially?

(After the lesson is completed) Show us the rabbit you made and tell us more about a rabbit you have seen before or one you know about from a story you have read. How does this rabbit differ from ones you've known about?

PRINTING SNOWFLAKES

Discovering a Way to Make Prints

You'll Need
Synthetic clay patties, about ½ in. thick, 3 in. wide, crayons or marker caps, thickly mixed white tempera paint, small containers for paint (watercolor cups or jar lids), small paint brushes, black construction paper 12 in. × 18 in., white paper 4 in. × 18 in., white glue or

paste, a copy of Lesley Anne Ivory's *Snow* (London: Burke Books, 1974) or an appropriate poem about snow.

Let's Go

Pick a snowy day! Read the book *Snow* to the children, or an appropriate poem about snow. Show the children how to tear the white paper down the middle. One of these torn pieces will be pasted on the bottom of their black paper to represent snow on the ground. The torn edge will look soft and fluffy on the black paper. Demonstrate to the children how they can make designs in their clay with the flat end of a crayon or marker cap. Then they can brush white paint onto the imprinted clay, and gently press the painted surfaces onto the black paper about three times without recharging the clay with more paint. Each "snowflake" will be different, some lighter, some darker. When the printed papers are dry, line them up side by side for a "world of snowflakes."

Artalk Artalk Artalk Artalk Artalk

Are snowflakes *ever* alike? Did you ever study a snowflake on your mitten or under a magnifying glass? Tell us about a snowy day that you remember. How many of you have been outside in the evening when the snow is softly falling? Can you tell us about it?

A FANTASY TREE

Learning Paper Sculpture Techniques

You'll Need
Rectangles, squares, circles, strips of poster paper in different colors and sizes, scissors, paste or white glue, old floor lamp, colored paper streamers.

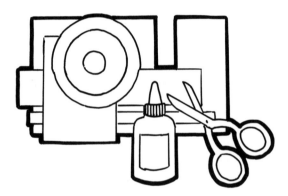

Let's Go
(Use the first of the Artalk questions now.) Demonstrate to the children how to make each of the three-dimensional forms illustrated on the facing page. Show them that a cone is made by slitting a circle or by rolling it out of a right triangle. A rectangular shape is made by folding a long strip into five equal sections and pasting the first section over the fifth. A cube is made by folding a wide strip into five equal sections that are exactly the same size as the width of the paper and pasting the first section over the fifth. (Use the second Artalk question now.) You can make a circular loop shape by bringing a strip around and pasting the ends together. (Use the third Artalk question now.) Spiral sections can be gathered and pasted so that the total form does not dangle. Accordion-pleated paper ends can be brought around to make a pleated circle. (Use the fourth Artalk question now.) The children

should pick one of the forms that they like and make several in that same shape. (Sizes and colors may vary, but the shape should be the same.) These should be connected into a cluster. (Use the fifth Artalk question now.) Tell the children to connect their clusters so that the shapes face in different directions. They can then tie strings at a good balance point for hanging. To make the "tree" the children can cover an old floor lamp with one color of crepe-paper streamers so that the identifying features are hidden (metal pole, paper shade). Let the children tie their clusters over the outside of the lamp, on the inside wires that brace the shade, and to the lamppost. Be sure that the paper clusters hang well away from the light bulb. Plug in the cord, turn on the switch, and let the children admire their "fantasy tree."

Artalk Artalk Artalk Artalk Artalk

1. What are some simple three-dimensional shapes you can make with your paper?
2. Can you think of a way to make a three-dimensional round shape?
3. What are some other ways to bend paper into a three-dimensional form?
4. A number of things growing together is sometimes called a cluster. What are some *clusters* we find in nature?

    grapes on a vine
    a honey comb
    petals on a flower
    leaves on a branch
    microscopic cell structures
    bubbles
    bare twigs on a branch

5. Can you think of some ways you can connect your cluster? Pasting sides together, interlocking slit ends, slitting ends and making tabs that can be pasted flat onto another flat surface.

(As the children are finishing) What do you think of our "tree"? How many of you think paper sculpture is hard to do? Which three-dimensional form is easiest to make? Which one was the hardest for you? Now that you've had some practice, would you like to try again sometime?

A DECORATIVE MASK

Learning More Paper Sculpture Techniques

You'll Need

Bright colors of construction paper (plus black and white) 9 in. × 12 in., scissors, staplers, clear adhesive tape, brightly colored paper scraps, glue or paste.

Let's Go

Tell the children that in many nations of the world the mask has been and still is a high art form. Let the children choose the colored paper they want for their masks. Show them how to slash the paper to make three different sculptured forms for a mask. Then they may add eyes, nose, and mouth by cutting into the paper or by using the paper sculpture techniques described in the lesson preceding this one. As they select colors for features, encourage them to repeat colors and shapes that will help make the mask look unified. Tabs and slits are helpful in making separate units fit together.

Artalk Artalk Artalk Artalk Artalk

Do you have a mask at home that you have worn on Halloween? Did you ever make a mask yourself? How did you do it? Have any of you ever seen masks at a museum that are made of wood or leather?

(As the children are finishing) Is anyone ready to show their mask? What was the hardest part about making the mask? What techniques did you use to make it look three-dimensional? Does it look the way you hoped it would? Is anyone disappointed with theirs? What do you think could make it better? Who'd like to make some suggestions?

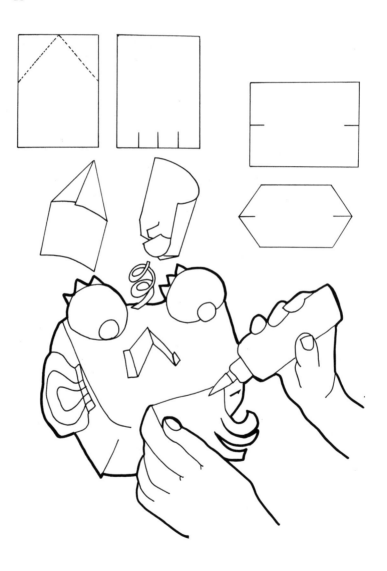

MAKING PORTRAITS

Learning the Proportions of the Face

You'll Need

Yellow construction paper 9 in. × 12 in., white drawing paper 9 in. × 12 in., newsprint 9 in. × 12 in., lead pencils, colored pencils or thin-line markers, crayons, white glue or paste, as many hand mirrors as available.

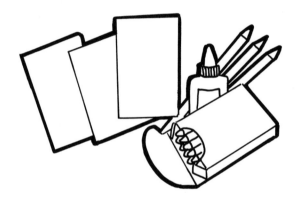

Let's Go

Use the Artalk questions first. Tell the children they may each draw a portrait of anyone they choose. On the newsprint paper they can practice. On a chalkboard or a large piece of paper taped to a wall, draw a large egg shape for a head. Using the span of a hand as a measure, let the children discover that the distance between the top of one's head and one's eyes is about the same as the distance between eyes and chin. To help locate the position of the ears on the head, tell the children to slide the side of a hand across their eyes. If they keep moving the hand in the same direction, the hand will brush the top of the ear. Likewise if they slide the side of a hand horizontally across the mouth, as the hand moves to the side of the head it will touch an ear lobe. Encourage the children to study the shape of the eye, the eyelid,

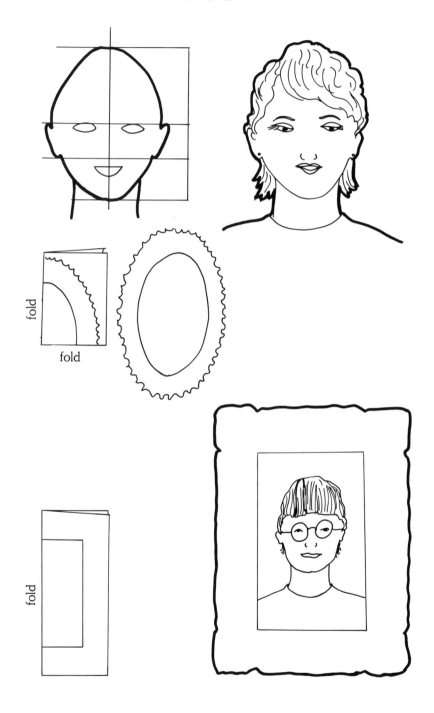

the lashes and eyebrows, by sharing hand mirrors. When they draw a mouth, they will need to define the separations between the lips, the edge of the top lip, and the edge of the bottom lip. A nose is hard to draw. Curved lines indicating the nostrils is all that is necessary. When the children begin to draw hair, point out to them that the hairline in front is well below the top of the head. Depending on hair style, front hair locks may fall forward covering much of the forehead. Tell the children to put a hand on each side of the neck and slide them up over each ear. They will discover that a neck is only slightly narrower than a head. Shoulders slope just a little.

As soon as the children are ready, have them begin making their portrait on their white drawing paper using colored pencils or crayons. If some of the children are bored by all of the restrictions of the proportions, let them make up a cartoon face or another face of their choice.

On another day, the children can make a "gold" frame for their portrait. If they want a rectangular frame, a good way to make it is to fold the yellow paper in half the long way and cut out a "window," leaving a two-inch border. An oval frame can be cut more evenly if the yellow paper is folded twice, and the open corners carefully rounded off in a smooth arc. While the frame is folded, the outside edges may be nicked or scalloped to create a decorative edge. After the frame is flattened out, "gold" decorations can be added with brown or orange markers or crayons. The frame can then be centered on the portrait, pasted down, and the edges of the portrait that go beyond the edges of the frame can be carefully trimmed.

Artalk Artalk Artalk Artalk Artalk

What is a portrait? How many of you have a portrait of someone in your home? Is it a photograph? Who is it a picture of? Has anyone ever seen a painted portrait of someone? Where did you see it? Sometimes at fairs or at shopping malls you can watch an artist drawing a portrait with charcoal or pastels. Have any of you ever seen one?

(As the children are finishing) Who is willing to show their portrait? Who is this supposed to be? What do you think of it? What parts of it are OK?

(If they are disappointed) What do you think is wrong with it? Does anyone have any suggestions?

ERASER PRINTS

Repeating a Shape to Make a Pattern

You'll Need

Colored construction paper 6 in. × 8 in., practice newsprint 6 in. × 8 in., art gum erasers 1 in. square, single-edged razor blades, water soluble printing ink, brayers, styrofoam trays, examples of fabric, wallpaper or wrapping paper with closely repeated patterns. (Set up printing stations with one brayer, one tube of the printing ink, and one styrofoam tray for every four children.)

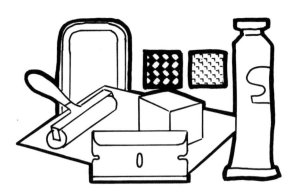

Let's Go

Use the Artalk questions first. Tell the children to use their pencils and rulers to make a light one-inch border all around both the practice newsprint and the colored construction paper. Then the children may draw, on the top of the eraser, a very simple shape touching all four edges. If they want to make an initial, remind them to draw it backwards, with lines at least 1/8″ thick. In order to print their design the children must cut away the empty areas so that the design is raised. With a word of caution in the use of razor blades,* demonstrate

---

*For safety's sake, distribute razor blades only when the designs are prepared for cutting. Enforce silence during cutting process. Collect razor blades as soon as the children are finished cutting.

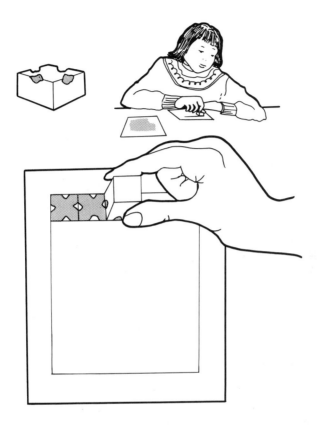

how to cut with the corner of the razor blade on the lines of their design about 1/8 of an inch into the art gum. Then show them how to carefully chip out small pieces from the empty areas, holding the blade at an angle.

When their printing "stamp" is ready, the children may go to a printing station. One child in each group can squeeze a small amount of water-soluble ink onto the styrofoam tray and roll the brayer back and forth in the ink until it feels tacky and is spread out evenly on the styrofoam tray. Each child can press the design into the ink "pad" and press it onto the practice newsprint, lining up the stamp so that the top and left side fit inside the top left corner of the penciled border. They should continue stamping so that each print touches the one behind it; when printing each succeeding row, the images should touch each other on top and bottom. There will be six rows of four images each. When they are ready they can proceed to print the image on "good" paper. If the ink starts to dry, a drop of water may be added and the brayer rolled over it to mix the water with the dried ink. When they are finished printing, they will notice how the empty spaces between the printed shapes make interesting patterns, too. These prints take several hours to dry, so provide an out-of-the-way place for storing.

Artalk Artalk Artalk Artalk Artalk

Look around you. Where can you find a repeated pattern? Look at your clothing. Now look around the room. Who can point out some patterns (floor tile, patterns on light fixtures, on book covers)? Name other places where patterns are repeated over and over (a brick wall, a window grate, windows in a skyscraper). What is a negative? In art the term "negative space" is the space left over after the design is made.

(As the children finish) Who is ready to show their eraser print pattern? Can you show us the single shape you started with? What do you think of your shape now that it's been repeated over and over? What does it remind you of? Do you notice how the negative spaces make shapes, too? What do you think of *that*?

MOONLIT SCENE

Learning How to Show Distance

You'll Need
Gray construction paper 9 in. × 12 in., white chalk, black thin-line markers.

Let's Go
Ask the children how they perceive the same object as it recedes in space. If they are going down a straight road in a car, what happens to the road in front of them? Write *foreground*, *middle ground*, and *background* on a blackboard or on a piece of paper big enough so the children can easily read it. They are to make pictures in which large

objects appear in the foreground (the lower third of the paper), middle-size objects appear in the middle ground (the middle of the paper), and very tiny objects appears in the background (such as trees, which can be suggested by simple up and down strokes with the marker), in the upper middle. They should draw a horizon line where the sky meets the ground. Tell the children that the foreground objects may project up

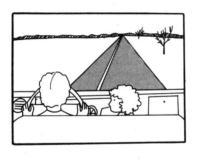

foreground

middleground

background

from lower area of the paper into the sky (such as trees, telephone poles, or tall buildings). They may place a moon in the sky with the white chalk and show moonlight on objects or the natural contours of the world below. Then they may try to show lights in windows (and the patterns these make on the ground outside). With their black markers they may also want to try to make shadows.

Artalk Artalk Artalk Artalk Artalk

How have you tried to show the illusion of distance in your picture? Tell us what is in the foreground, middle ground, and background. Did you make highlights or shadows? Do you feel fairly successful in creating this illusion?

(For those who are disappointed) What do you think is wrong with your picture? Who can suggest an idea to make it better?

CARDBOARD DIORAMA

Learning About Overlapping

You'll Need
White tagboard 12 in. × 18 in., photographs of landscapes, of scenes underwater, in space, or any appropriate for backgrounds. (Pictures should be large enough to cover the upper half of the tagboard.) Good sources: *National Geographic, Arizona Highways, Wisconsin Trails, Modern Maturity*, travel magazines, crayons, scraps of tagboard for stand-up objects and figures, scissors, paste or white glue, pencils.

Let's Go
Use the Artalk questions first. Give each child a "background" to paste to the upper half of the tagboard (1). If the picture doesn't quite cover, color in the rest of the picture, trying to duplicate as closely as

possible the shapes and colors in the photograph. Now the children may fold the tagboard (2), creating a diorama illusion. The children will now decide what to draw and color in the foreground which will fit with the background scene (3), after discussing ways of drawing roads, streams, and so on to make them appear as though they recede. Stress careful application and blending of the crayons to enhance the illusion of space. This much might be enough for one art class. On another day, the children may use scraps of tagboard to make stand-up figures and objects in proper proportion to each other and the background (4). The children should make at least three stand-up objects or figures and place them at various positions from the front edge to the background scene. Be sure the children remember to cut a tab at the bottom of each figure. This tab will be folded under and pasted. The stand-ups should not exceed four inches in height or they will tend to sag.

Artalk Artalk Artalk Artalk Artalk

What can you make or draw to give the illusion of distance? After some discussion, the children should have responded with the following:

- place things so they overlap
- make objects smaller in the distance
- use softer colors for things in the distance
- show lots of details in things close up

If the children name fewer than the four techniques listed, provide them with this information.

(As the children finish) Who is ready to show their diorama? Show us what you did to create the feeling of distance. Do you think it "works"? Which part of your diorama do you think is the best? Is there any part you are dissatisfied with? Move away from your diorama and look at it. From a distance the illusion is greater, isn't it?

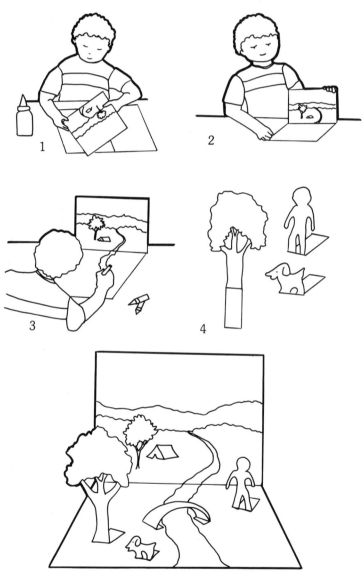

MAKING A SLOGAN

Learning to Cut Letters

You'll Need

Strips of newsprint 3 in. ✕ 18 in., strips of colored construction paper 3 in. ✕ 18 in., strips of colored construction paper 5 in. ✕ 18 in., scissors, pencils, rulers, white paste or glue.

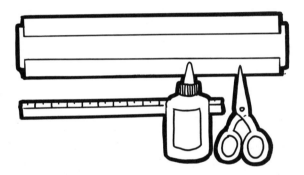

Let's Go

Use the Artalk questions first. Tell the children to fold the newsprint until it is divided into eighths, then cut the pieces apart on the folds. Use the chart to show them how to cut each letter from the resulting rectangles. When cutting parallel to a fold, remember that when the fold is opened the cut area will be double in size. The children should observe that all the lines of each letter are the same thickness; as they cut areas away, watch that the remaining shapes are consistent in width.

Ask each child to choose background strips that contrast in color with the letters. On these larger construction-paper strips, guidelines, one inch from the top and from the bottom edges can be drawn. Then the children may trace the letters they have cut out for their slogan onto the three-inch construction paper, cut these out, and paste them between the guidelines. Start at least two inches from the

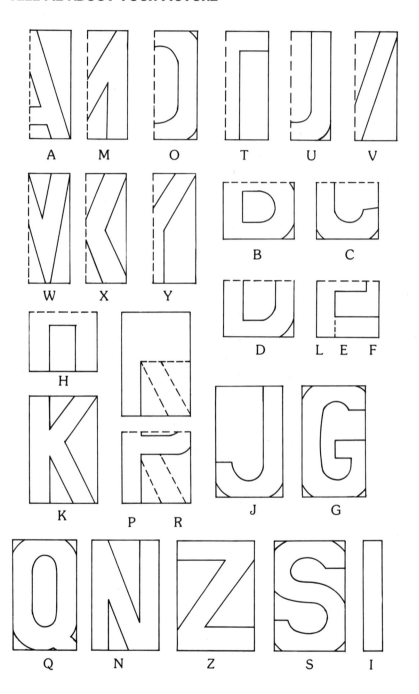

left edge of the paper. Extra space on the right can be trimmed to center the slogan.

Artalk Artalk Artalk Artalk Artalk

What is a slogan? Think of some slogans that we all know (Be Prepared, Drink Milk, Have a Nice Day, Don't Litter, Drive Slow). Can you think of a slogan that is eight letters or less? (Enjoy, Peace, Be Happy, Love, Exercise, Go Team). If you can't think of a slogan, you may want to cut the letters of your name, of our school, or our town (or abbreviations if there are too many letters).

(When they are finished) Tell us why you chose that particular slogan.

MAKING CURVED SHAPES LOOK REAL

Implying Three Dimensions Through Value Change

You'll Need

Gray construction paper 12 in. × 18 in., charcoal pencils, white chalk, standard writing pencils, playground ball, wastebasket, side light sources (windows, projector lamp, spotlight), facial tissues.

Let's Go

Set the ball and an overturned wastebasket side by side on an empty table so that the ball rests against the basket. Turn off any overhead lights and let your windows provide the light. If you do not have windows, use a projector light or spotlight to illuminate one side of each object. Let the children move about so that all can see clearly. Tell the children to turn their papers in the direction that seems appropriate and sketch each object lightly with their pencils. The objects should be

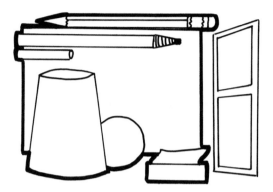

drawn large so that they fill the space. Use the Artalk questions now. Tell the children to squint their eyes and look for the lightest spots on the ball and the basket. They should press hard with their white chalk when drawing these areas. Now have them look for the darkest places on the ball and basket, and color these heavily with charcoal pencil. Now they must blend the white into the black so there are no perceivable divisions in the surfaces. They can start by coloring lightly with chalk around white areas. This will result in a soft gray color. Then they can gently tone the areas near the dark places with charcoal pencils. They should let the charcoal tone become lighter and lighter until it meets the gray of the chalk. Facial tissue will help blend the tones evenly.

Artalk Artalk Artalk Artalk Artalk

Where is the lightest spot on the ball? Someone come and point to the place where it seems lightest. Where is the lightest place on the basket? Now where is the darkest place on the ball and basket? Is it on the rim of the basket? Is it on an area of the ball? Is it on the bottom? Someone else come and show us where you think it is.

(As the children are finishing) You're going to be amazed when you see how good these look! Who is ready to show theirs? (Tell each child to lean the picture against some books or on a chalk ledge.) Step back so that you can view it from a distance. Now, what do you think of it? What makes it look real?

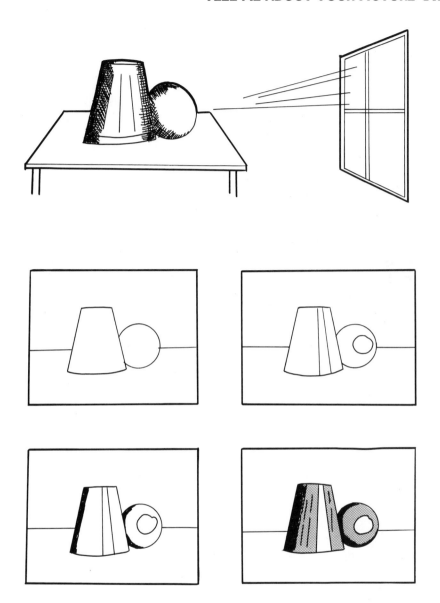

12

TELL ME ABOUT "TRICKS" YOU CAN DO WITH ART MATERIALS

A medium new to the children takes them exploring unknown paths. Household items such as aluminum foil and waxed paper, combined with standard art media, spark new interest. Using an iron, a paper bag, colored tissue paper, or clear acetate in an art lesson inspires curiosity and a desire to touch and try. To some children who have fallen into the "can't" syndrome, the appearance of these unusual materials can be diverting. If specific directions are given and innovative goals are set, some children who have grown tired of traditional approaches to making things or who balk at risking failure may be inspired to try once more. An unfamiliar medium or a familiar medium used in a new way calls for responses different from those of the past, so that previous "goofs" hold no power. Novel materials may lack depth but they can provide a child with a bag of tricks with which he can be impressed, at least temporarily. Such experiences can build the courage that in time will motivate the child to master a variety of skills and concepts that hold more challenge.

The response to these new experiences can be wonder, delight, surprise, and a desire to talk. Gentle persuasion can ease the aloof youngster into conversation about each new experience and each refreshing, new success.

Comments might be, "Were you surprised by what you did? That looks pretty neat! I bet you didn't think you would like it, did you?

Why don't you tell us how you created that effect?" or "Wow, that is really terrific! How in the world did you do that? C'mon, let us in on how you did it! We really want to know!"

Even though they may be secretly pleased with their success, some children may show mock dismay or feign indifference when you urge them to show and tell about their pictures. More than a little urging may be necessary to pry them away from this resolute stance. They have to be absolutely convinced that you really want to see and hear about what they have accomplished.

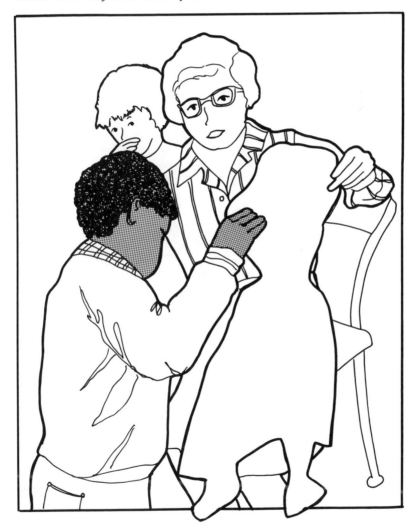

SPRING RABBITS

Learning to Use a Pattern

You'll Need

White drawing paper 6 in. × 9 in., colorfully patterned gift wrapping paper pieces 3 in. × 5 in., scissors, white glue or paste, crayons or colored markers, pencils, solid-color paper scraps

Let's Go

Use the Artalk questions first. Show the children how simple it is to draw a cartoon-like rabbit. The tip of the ears should touch the top of the paper, the forepaws should touch the sides, and the feet should touch the bottom. If they start drawing with a circle shape as big as a fist, and attach ears that touch the top, they are well on their way to success. If they make the rabbit too small, encourage them to try again on the back. After they have made a rabbit that suits them, they can outline it with colored marker or crayon, then cut it out on the lines. Now they should select a decorative paper for a jacket or other clothing. You should demonstrate how to position the decorative paper behind the rabbit so that the lines of the clothing can be drawn to fit the body. Some children may prefer simply to cut slices of paper and fold them around the body for coats or sleeves, cutting small pieces to fill the shoulder area. The children will find their own way. They may want to make collars, ties, shoes, and mitts as well, so bring out colored scraps for these.

Artalk Artalk Artalk Artalk Artalk

How many of you like new clothes? Does someone in your family make clothes for you? Is it fun to have new clothes in the spring? Tell us about a time you wore a new shirt or dress.

(After the lesson is finished) Show us the new clothes you made for your rabbit. Perhaps we can have a fashion parade of our rabbits if we fasten them two by two up on a wall.

PAPER BAG ANIMALS

Using a Paper Bag as a Form

You'll Need

White paper bags size 8, newspaper, tempera paint (orange, brown, gray, white, black), clear tape, staplers, cotton (for rabbit tails), colored markers, construction paper (brown, gray, white), scissors, school paste.

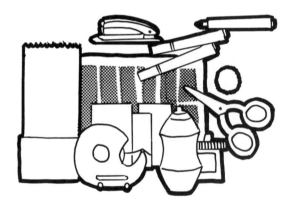

Let's Go

Each child is to crush lightly two double sheets of newspaper and stuff them loosely in a bag. Each should carefully close the bag and tape it smoothly shut so it is rounded on top. Let the children choose the color of animal they want to make and paint the top and sides of the bag; let dry. Tell the children that the animals have to be sitting on haunches.

On another day, start out with the Artalk questions. After the discussion, suggest ways to fold paper for ears and paws. Suggest ways to attach these pieces.

Artalk Artalk Artalk Artalk Artalk

Did any of you ever have a stuffed animal when you were little? What did you have? A teddy bear, a panda, a dog, a cat, a rabbit? How many of you have one now? What is a way you can attach ears and a tail onto the body form? (Fold a tab at the end of each cut piece and paste it onto the bag.) What will be the best way to make faces on your animal? (Draw with colored marker or cut out colored construction paper features and paste these on.)

(As the children are finishing) Who would like to show their animal and tell something about it? Who else would like to show us their animal? Is the animal you made something like your pet? Is the animal something like an animal you would like to own?

FISHBOWLS

Using Waxed Paper to Create an Illusion

You'll Need
Colored tissue paper scraps, waxed paper 12 in. × 18 in., scissors, iron, newspaper, colored construction paper scraps, manila paper 12 in. × 18 in.

Let's Go
Let's make a fishbowl! Tell the children to fold the waxed paper in half. The folded edge will be the bottom of the fish tank. They should lay their folded paper on their manila paper for support. Keeping the waxed paper folded, they may want to trim the sides if they would like a rounded bowl instead of a tank. (Use the Artalk questions now.)

When they cut the images to go in their fish tank or bowl, they may use the tissue paper or the construction paper to cut out their fish, seaweed, etc. Cutting things out of tissue paper will enhance a "see-through" effect, but if it is too difficult for the children to cut, tell them that the construction paper will work, too. When they have cut out all their pieces, they should position them inside the folded waxed paper and carefully carry the manila paper "tray" to an ironing station. There should be a generous layer of newspapers underneath and one layer on top, which should be changed after the iron is pressed over each fish bowl to seal it. The iron should be set on "warm" or "permanent press." If it is too hot the waxed paper will not seal. These fish bowls may be affixed in windows with clear tape for an attractive display.

Artalk Artalk Artalk Artalk Artalk

How many of you have ever seen a fish in a fishbowl? Where did you see it? What are some things that you see in a fishbowl besides fish (castle, marbles, coral, seaweed, treasure chest). You might even decide to make some things that might be found in water, but not in fishbowls (such as miniature divers, submarines, or mermaids).

(As the children are finishing) Who would like to show us and tell us about the fishbowl they made? What interesting things have you added to make it different from a real one? Would you like to *own* a fishbowl such as the one you are showing us? Who has a different "cast of characters" to show?

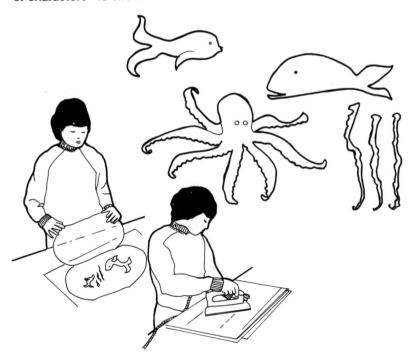

MAGIC PAINTING

Making a Watercolor Wash over White Crayon

You'll Need

60 lb. white drawing paper 9 in. × 12 in., one set of eight-pan watercolors, container for water, watercolor brush size eight or larger, white crayon, one of each for each child.

Let's Go

Tell the children to dip the paintbrush in water, and put a drop of water in each of their eight paint pans. Then the children should think of a picture they would like to make that has lots of details. A good choice is one large object in which there are many shapes, such as a clown, a boat, a fish, a car, a vase of flowers or a butterfly. They should press hard with their white crayons on the white paper to make the outline and then draw in the details, again pressing hard. It will not be difficult to see what they are drawing, because the wax in the crayon will shine on the paper. Now the children may gently wash their papers with water, sweeping their wet brush lightly over the paper until it is saturated. Next they should dip the brush in one of the lightest colors, loading the brush with color, and paint three swatches of color in

different areas of the wet paper. They should repeat this procedure two more times, with other colors. The colors will mingle together. The children should select one more color to fill in the empty spaces. They should hold their paintbrushes loosely as they rapidly paint the white areas before the water dries. As they apply each color, the white crayon will appear like magic, the wax in the crayon resisting the watercolor washes. Some children may want to tilt the paper back and forth to further blend colors, but they may be disappointed in the results if the colors run together too much.

Artalk Artalk Artalk Artalk Artalk

What new colors did you make? Who knows why the crayon resists the watercolor? What do you think of this technique? Would you like to try it again?

STYROFOAM BUTTERFLIES

Making a Mural with Styrofoam Prints

You'll Need

One printing station should be set up for every four children. They should be supplied with water-soluble printing ink (any color), a flat surface to roll the ink on, such as glass (edges must be taped), cardboard, or a magazine taped shut; a brayer, newsprint sheets cut 4½ in. × 6 in., as well as several colors of construction paper or colored newsprint 4½ in × 6 in. Yellow mural paper (size to be determined by the number of children participating) should be attached to a wall at eye level where the children can work. (Use the floor if no smooth wall surface is nearby.) The children should each have a Styrofoam meat tray at least 4 in. × 6 in., a pencil, scissors, and school paste or white glue. Colored paper scraps should be available.

Let's Go

Use the Artalk questions first. Tell the children to trim the lip of the meat tray so that the whole surface is flat. They should use the side of the tray that has no impression in it. They are to draw a butterfly large enough so that the sides of the wings meet the edges of the tray. It is perhaps best to make a tube-like shape first for the body and then add the wings on each side. The children then can press with their pencils to add decorative lines and swirls inside the wings and body. Now they should cut out their butterfly, being careful to proceed slowly in hard-to-get-places, as the Styrofoam breaks easily. Antennae must be drawn wide enough so they don't break during the cutting. Now the children may each go to a printing station. The teacher or leader should squeeze a small amount of the ink onto each printing surface, and one child from each group can roll the brayer back and forth in the ink until it feels and sounds tacky. Now each child in turn can roll the inked brayer over the butterfly, and then carefully press the inked surface onto a trial piece of newsprint. The print will be more successful if the child then flips the paper with the inked Styrofoam so that the paper is on top. A light pressing with the fingers will then make a clearer print. The lines drawn with their pencils will show in the color of the paper. They should peel off the paper carefully in one motion. They may want to practice printing a few times until they get a satisfactory print. Then they may select a piece of colored construction paper and make a print to be used on the mural. If there is time, they may want to print one more to take home. Water-soluble ink takes several hours to dry, so assembling the mural can be left to another day. When the children cut out their butterflies for the mural, they should leave a little space between the printed edge and the colored paper for an attractive border. Then they can paste their butterflies onto the yellow mural paper. Those who finish first might cut out flowers, leaves, and stems to line the bottom of the mural.

Artalk Artalk Artalk Artalk Artalk

Did any of you ever see a butterfly collection? Butterflies are a popular subject for art because each has its own shape with varying patterns in the wings. Does someone know an easy way to draw a butterfly? Come to the chalkboard (or to a paper mounted on a flat surface) and show us. Would someone else like to show a different way? Do butterflies have two or four wings? Yes, some have two and some have four. What are some patterns you can draw on the wings? You can make your patterns as complex as you wish. Our printing technique will show every detail you draw.

(After the butterflies have been attached to the mural) Who would like to go to the mural and show us their butterfly? Are you pleased with the way your butterfly turned out? Are there lines you wish you had added? Where would they go?

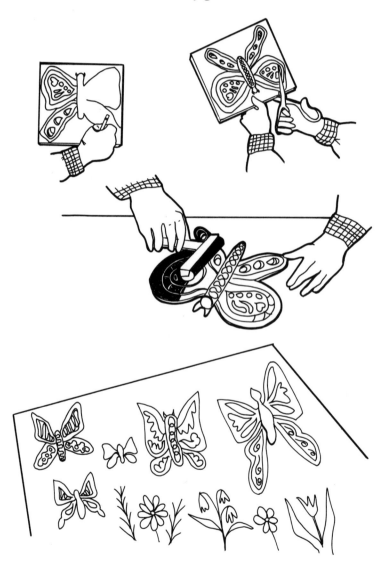

ACTION PICTURES

Learning Art Tricks to Show Movement

You'll Need
Colored tissue paper, 10 colors 3 in. × 5 in., small watercolor brushes, scissors, white drawing paper 9 in. × 12 in., white glue, manila drawing paper 3 in. × 5 in.

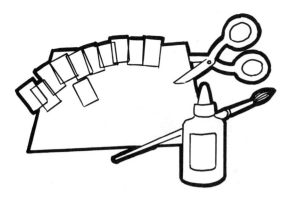

Let's Go
Use the Artalk questions first. The children should draw the subject they have chosen on the manila drawing paper. Remind them that the subject should be identified by its shape only, and that drawing inside the shapes would spoil the moving illusion. Then they may cut out the silhouette and trace it onto one of the sheets of colored tissue. Next, gathering all the sheets of tissue underneath, they should carefully cut all ten pieces of paper at once. The paper will drape over their hands, but if they cut slowly and keep a firm grasp, turning the paper as they cut, the task can be done easily. The paper is so thin that the cutting is easy. Next the children should decide how to arrange the pieces. They may want to overlap each piece in a sweeping arc (such as a fish), on a diagonal (such as a diver), or in an up/down fashion (such as a hopping rabbit), depending on the subject.

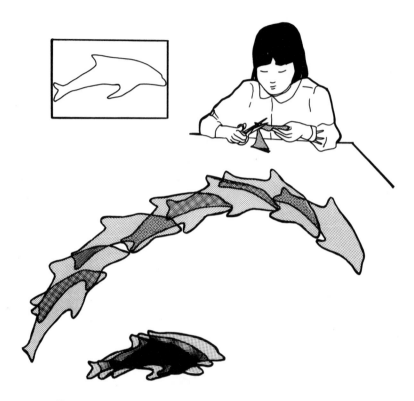

Encourage the children to be sensitive to the colors that are blended as new colors are overlapped. Once they have determined the order of overlapping, they should take off all the pieces and glue them in order of overlapping. They should lay the first piece in position on white paper, then brush the thinned white glue on top of it, starting in the middle and fanning out on every side to the white paper underneath. They should proceed in order with the next piece until all are secured.

Artalk Artalk Artalk Artalk Artalk

Did you ever see photographs of athletes in motion, or of car races, which show overlapping views of the action in one picture? You are going to do something like that today with overlapped pieces of colored tissue paper. Who can name some good action subjects for the pictures? What can you make that moves? What hops? What flies? What swims?

(As the children are finishing) Who is ready to talk about the action they have shown in their picture? How did you happen to think of your idea? Do you think your picture captures the illusion of movement that you hoped it would? If you look at it from a distance, you may be surprised by the movement that becomes clear. Who else is ready to show us their picture?

MOIRÉ LETTERS

Showing Movement as a Quality in Design

You'll Need
White drawing paper 6 in. × 9 in., color thin-line markers (any color except yellow), pencils, pieces of clear acetate 6 in. × 9 in. for each child.

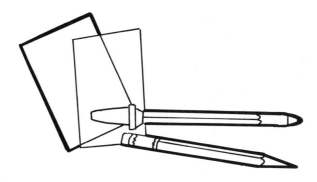

Let's Go
Ask the children to print their names lightly with a pencil so that the lines meet all sides of the white paper. They should go over the lines with a marker. To create an optical effect, they are to outline with the marker each of the original letter lines, over and over, larger and larger, until the entire space is filled. It is important that no lines cross or touch each other. There should be an equal distance between each line. To create the moiré illusion, have the children place an acetate sheet over

the pattern and trace it. When the completed pattern on the acetate is moved on top of the first design, a moiré effect is created.

Artalk Artalk Artalk Artalk Artalk

Let the children gather closely around a table and take turns showing how their moiré pattern "works." The artalk will flow naturally without assistance.

MOONSCAPE

Building Interesting Textures

You'll Need

Stiff cardboard circle 9 in. wide, tongue depressor, India ink, watercolor brush, piece of lightweight aluminum foil 12 in. square, small three-dimensional objects, masking tape for each child.

Let's Go

Use the Artalk questions first. Tell the children to tape a pleasing arrangement of three-dimensional objects onto the cardboard circle. They can use chunks of cardboard, wadded aluminum foil, nuts, bolts, screws, bottle caps or heavy cord. When satisfied with the arrangement, they should center the aluminum foil over the cardboard, and, starting from the center, press the foil closely around each raised form, working out to the edges. Creases resulting from the gathering around the raised objects will become part of the texture. At the edges, remaining foil should be folded tightly and taped underneath. India ink can be brushed over the entire area. When dry, the ink on the high areas may be gently scraped off with a tongue depressor, leaving a dramatic presentation of a textured pattern.

Artalk Artalk Artalk Artalk Artalk

What does the moon look like on the surface? Who has seen pictures of the moon's surface on TV, through a telescope or in a book? Are there mountains on the moon? Are there craters on the moon? Who can describe one? The surface of the moon is full of interesting textures. We are going to recreate a kind of textured surface that will be enjoyable to look at as well as to touch.

(As the children are finishing) Who is ready and eager to show us their "Moonscape"? What are some of the objects you chose to build up the form? Did anyone discover an interesting way to crease the foil to create more texture effects? What do you think about the effect of the India ink? Does it provide contrast to the aluminum foil?

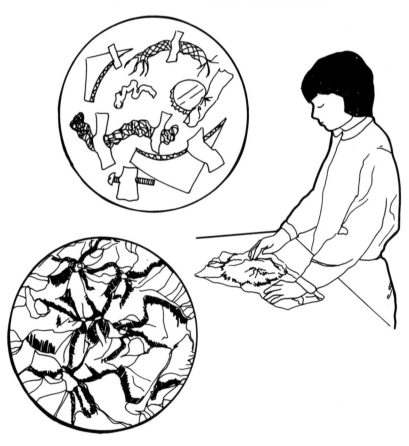

ONE-POINT PERSPECTIVE: NAMES

Learning to Draw Lines to a Vanishing Point

You'll Need
Graph paper with ¼ in. squares, pencils, colored thin-line markers.

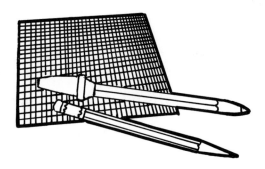

Let's Go
Use the Artalk questions first. Each child should choose a name, nickname, or slang expression to draw in perspective (the word must have no more than seven letters). Every letter should be five blocks wide (except the letter *i*) and six blocks high. The lines of each letter should be one block thick. To space the letters evenly, the children should place the middle letter of the word to be printed in the lower middle of the paper and work out to each side from there.

Two blocks should be left between each letter. Have them place a dot near the top edge of the paper about halfway across. To make the perspective projections, the trick is simply to draw lines from every corner of every letter to the dot except in cases where the line would penetrate the letter. The children may use their markers to fill in the letters or color the projections.

Artalk Artalk Artalk Artalk Artalk

Who knows what the word "perspective" means? Who remembers how to draw things so that they appear to be far away? Has anyone ever heard of the word "vanishing point"? An artist uses a vanishing point to help show deep space on a flat plane. (Show illustration) See how your eye is fooled into thinking that the letters move back into deep space.

    (As the children are finishing) Who is ready to show their perspective picture? Do you think this system really shows the feeling of space? Did the colors you chose to fill in your letters and projections *help* that feeling of space?

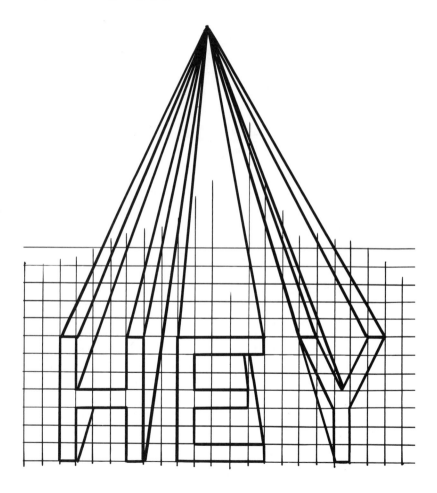

ONE-POINT PERSPECTIVE: A ROOM

Adding Imagination to Rules of Perspective

You'll Need

Manila drawing paper 9 in. × 12 in., pencils, colored thin-line markers, scissors, school paste, straightedge or ruler, magazines with colored advertisements or illustrations.

Let's Go

Tell the children to place a dot near the middle of the paper, and a rectangle around it about 3 in. × 4 in., sides parallel to the edges of the paper. They will establish perspective lines of ceiling and floor by projecting lines connecting the center dot (the vanishing point) and the corners of the small rectangle to the sides of the paper. Show them how to make windows in the sides of the room. The top and bottom lines will be slanted toward the dot to give them perspective. The children may also draw one large window in the back wall.

Now they may look in their magazines for objects or people who can be seen through the windows. These can be pasted onto the paper in appropriate positions. If they wish, the objects or people can be either very large or very small. The children might even find a foot that could project from outside to the inside, or the nose of an airplane. Encourage them to use imagination. They may decorate their room any way they wish with colored markers. Remind them that objects in back of the room should be smaller than those in the front.

Artalk Artalk Artalk Artalk Artalk

Show us your room and what you added for an interesting effect. Make up a story to explain your fantastic additions!

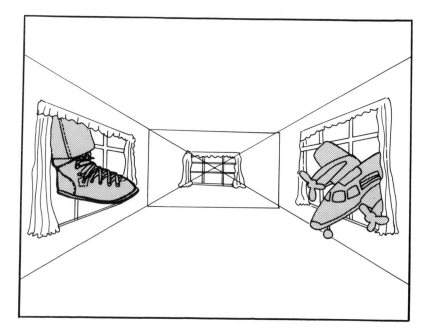

HEEL AND TOE PAINTING

Learning a Watercolor Technique

You'll Need

Eight-pan semi-moist watercolor sets, watercolor brushes, paper towels, white drawing paper 9 in. × 12 in., a generous container of water for each child, examples of Japanese sumi painting, if available.

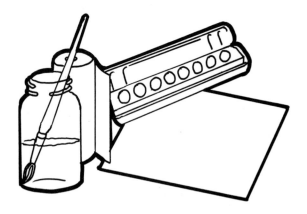

Let's Go

Tell the children it is fun to explore various watercolor techniques. One technique, a little like Japanese sumi painting, is called heel and toe painting. Show the children examples of Japanese sumi painting, if you have them, before you proceed. Instruct the children to put a drop of water on each of the eight watercolor pans in their sets. Then, gather the children around you and demonstrate how to (1) charge the brush with water, (2) lay the brush flat against a cake of moist watercolor, pressing the *heel* of the brush into the color and then (3) lift the brush and place the tip (or "toe") of the brush with a contrasting color. Now lay the bristles of the brush, charged with the two colors, flat onto a paper towel and lift straight up from the paper. It is possible to "print" in this manner several times before recharging the brush. Brown paper towels work well as practice paper. Let the children experiment with the heel and toe technique and any other printing techniques they would like to try. When they feel ready, have them start on the white paper, making pictures or designs and applying the paint in a manner of their choice.

Artalk Artalk Artalk Artalk Artalk

Show us the technique that worked well for you. What color combinations did you try? Which combinations do you like best? Tell us about the painting you made using your technique.

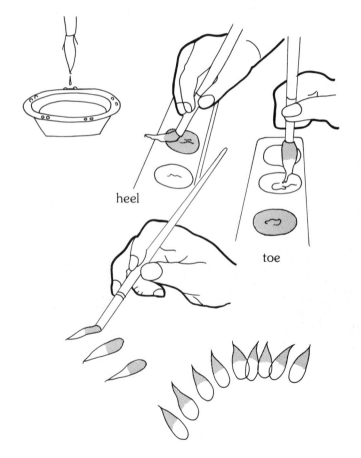

heel

toe

Index